How To Draw
Warriors
Of
Fantasy

BY FRANK GRANADOS

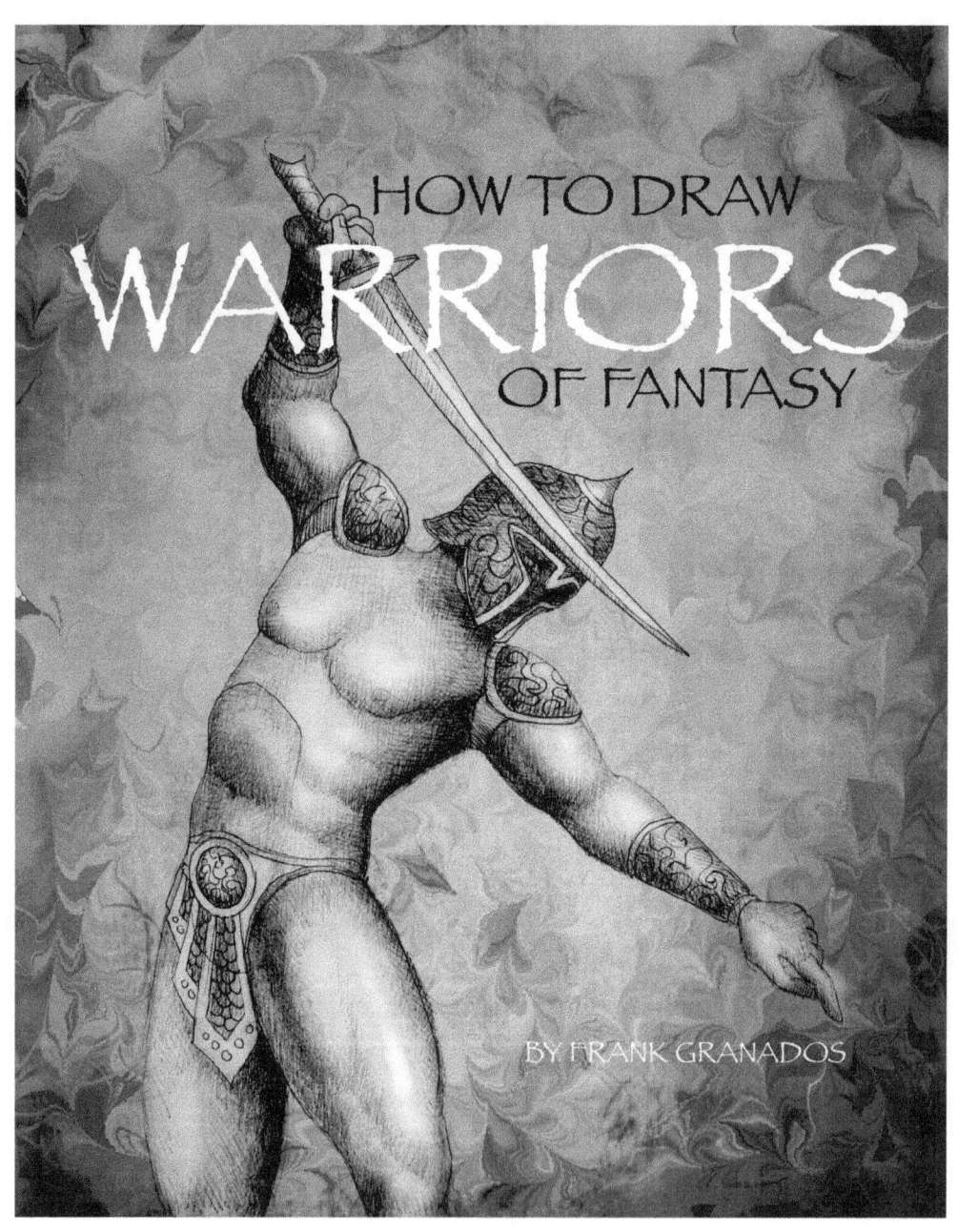

HOW TO DRAW
WARRIORS
OF FANTASY

BY FRANK GRANADOS

To Angel

Copyright

Deep within the caverns of the abyss lurk the beautiful eyes of the dragon. For it waits and watches for it's chance to feed on the vile flesh of humanity.

As we dare to enter into the endless labyrinth of time. We lose the fragile sense of who we are. Surrounded by the fear of darkness we become its prey.

We are beguiled into following the enchanted sounds of the echoes that lead us into its dominion. We hear the songs that are sung by the lost souls devoured by the dragon.

In the shadow of its existence it is hard to resist looking into the beautiful eyes of thc bcast.

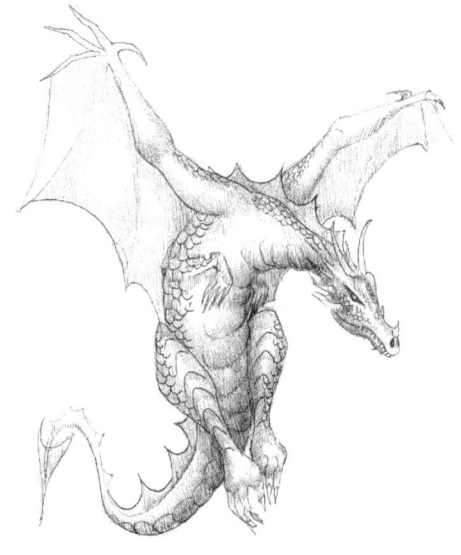

Table of contents

Foreword

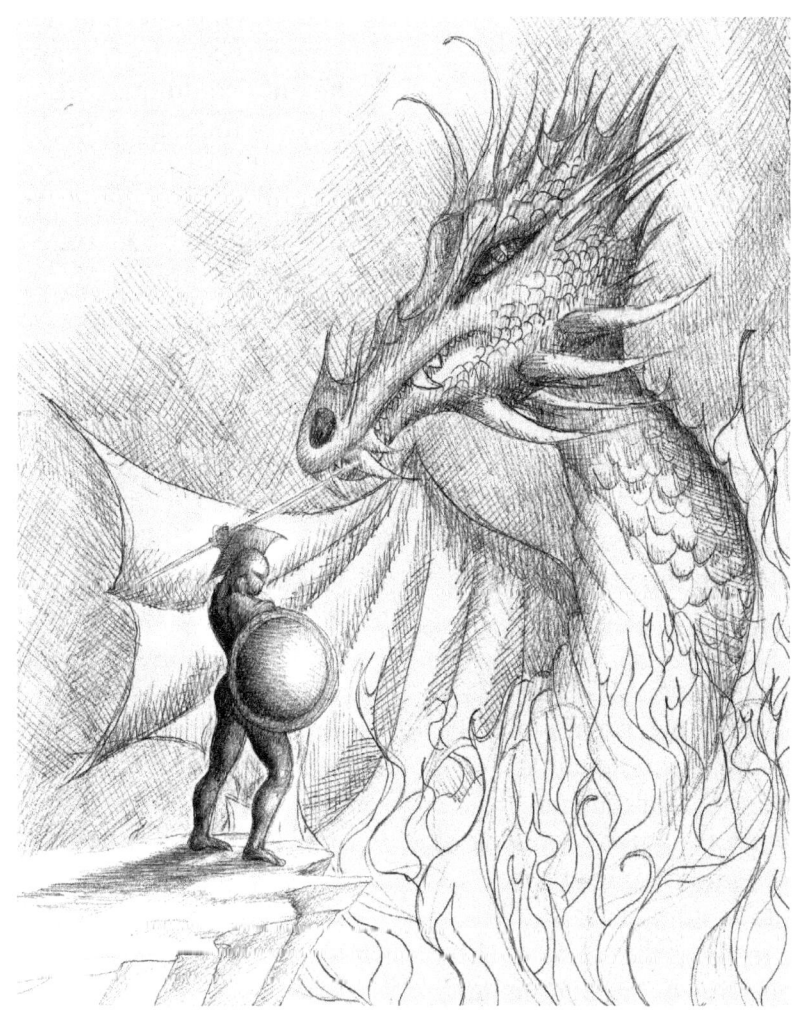

When I was a boy, back in west Texas, my father would tell me stories about dragons and warriors. Since then I have always loved fantasy art and stories. My favorite story was the one about Vigo and the Dragon.

From the depths of the abyss arose a great dragon and his breath rained fire and the blue skies of the desolate lands were turned into hues of crimson red. Day and night the dragon flew above the little village waiting and watching for its chance to feed on the villagers that he saw below. He spewed balls of fire above their heads and the flames burned the souls of those who cowered and hide behind the village walls. The dragon was unrelenting as he hunted their flesh and drank their blood. The dragon became intoxicated with the scent of their fears as he spread his wings and soared in ecstasy.

Rumors were spread by the voices in the fog of a great warrior who would fight and defeat the terrible dragon. A brave and fearless warrior named Vigo with the strength and courage to face the beast soon appeared. And he ventured to the underworld of the great abyss where the dragon and many evil and terrible creatures lurked.

Once there, Vigo entered the mouth of the abyss and he could see a huge pit about 100 meters across. There were flames shooting straight up into the thick and polluted atmosphere inside. Sharpe jagged ledges lead all the way down into the huge pit, they almost looked like giant steps. There was searing heat being generated from the fiery depth below. Vigo heard lamenting screams coming from below and he only could imagine what kind of torture must be going on.

He put his sword behind him and began to climb down. At first he had to jump down onto each ledge because of how steep the ledges were. The ledges were extremely jagged and they became very slippery because there was some kind of dark red liquid flowing down the ledges. Vigo had to be extremely careful not to slip or he would fall. The flames were also getting stronger and grew more violent and treacherous as he descended deeper into the abyss. Vigo finally reached the bottom ledge but he was extremely exhausted and felt the need to rest for a bit.

He looked out over the last ledge and he saw an opening into a large cavern and he decided to climb into it. It seemed as if he had been walking for hours as he explored the interior of the cave. It was dark and cold and damp unlike the rest of the abyss. Vigo could see these huge formations with glowing

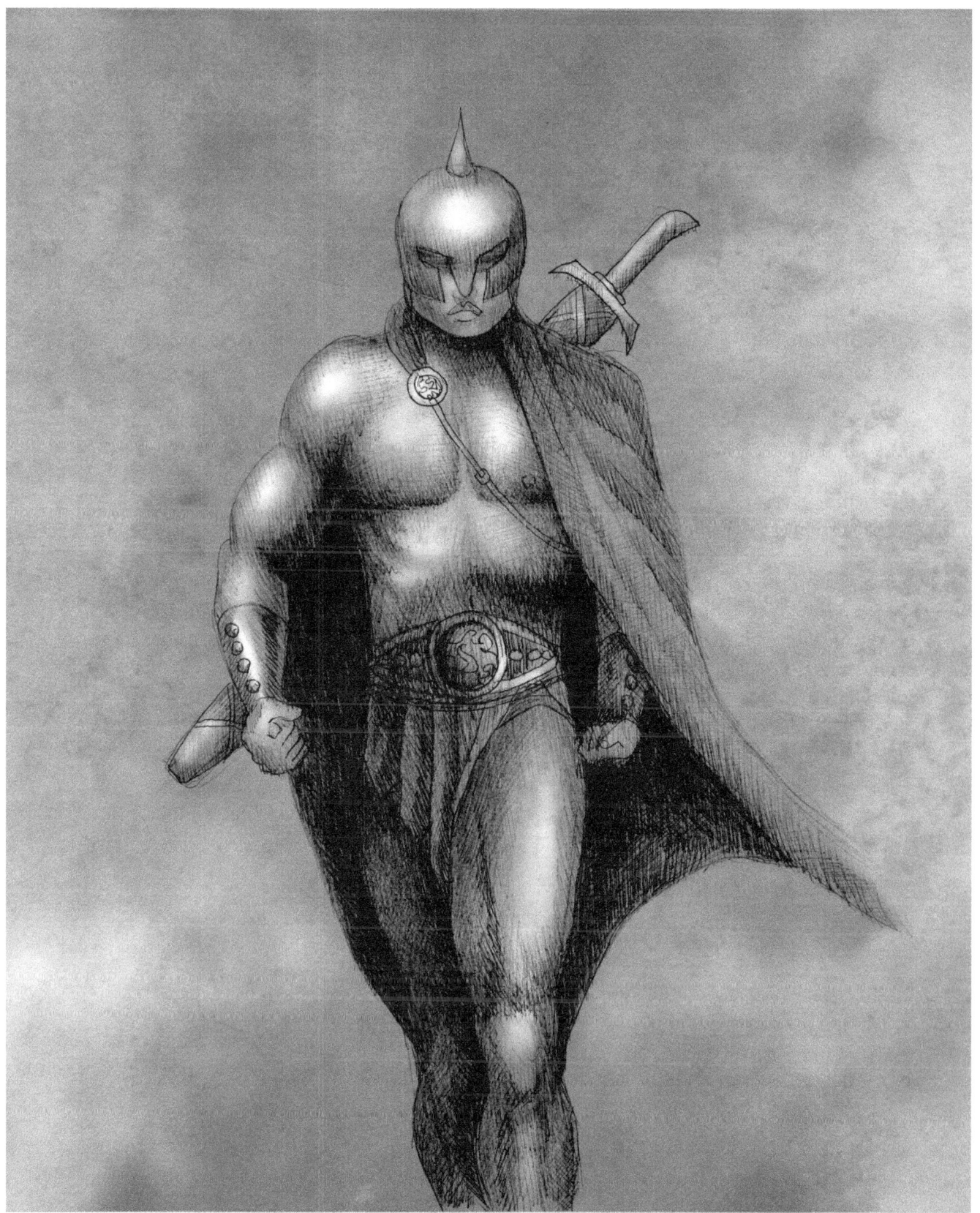

embers coming down from the ceiling. They looked like giant stalagmites glowing and pulsating with some sort of energy. Every few minutes, colorful sparks would shoot out and the whole cavern would be visible. Vigo could see the walls all covered in roots and strange looking vines and the floor was covered in a green mist.

He saw millions of tiny black wiggly creatures coming out of the mist and they were crawling as fast as they could up and down the walls. The creatures had tiny red blinking eyes and when they opened their mouths you could see small fangs dripping with saliva. They were using their fangs to suck up the strange red fluid that covered everything in the place.

Suddenly, one of the little creatures spotted Vigo and it instantly began blinking and flashing its hideous eyes like it was some kind of warning alarm. The little thing looked like it was going mad as it began to wiggle like crazy then it opened its tiny mouth and out popped its fangs as it started to chase him. Vigo decided to get out of there as fast as he could before the rest of the creatures came after him.

In the next cavern he could see a huge pool of red liquid with flames coming out of its center. Suddenly he heard a loud and thunderous roar and he looked up. A huge dragon covered in scales that looked like sharp razor blades sticking out of its spine glared at him. It was the one who was spewing the flames from the pit. The dragon was wrapped around a huge object that was shaped like a rectangle............

The preceding was a short preview of the book
Vigo And The Dragon.

As he stood among the death and the slaughter the dragon had left in its path. He felt the wind and the dust as it blew over the bones and scattered the ashes of those who had fallen. He made the vow to return if ever he was needed. He turned towards the wind and slowly faded into the sandstorm.

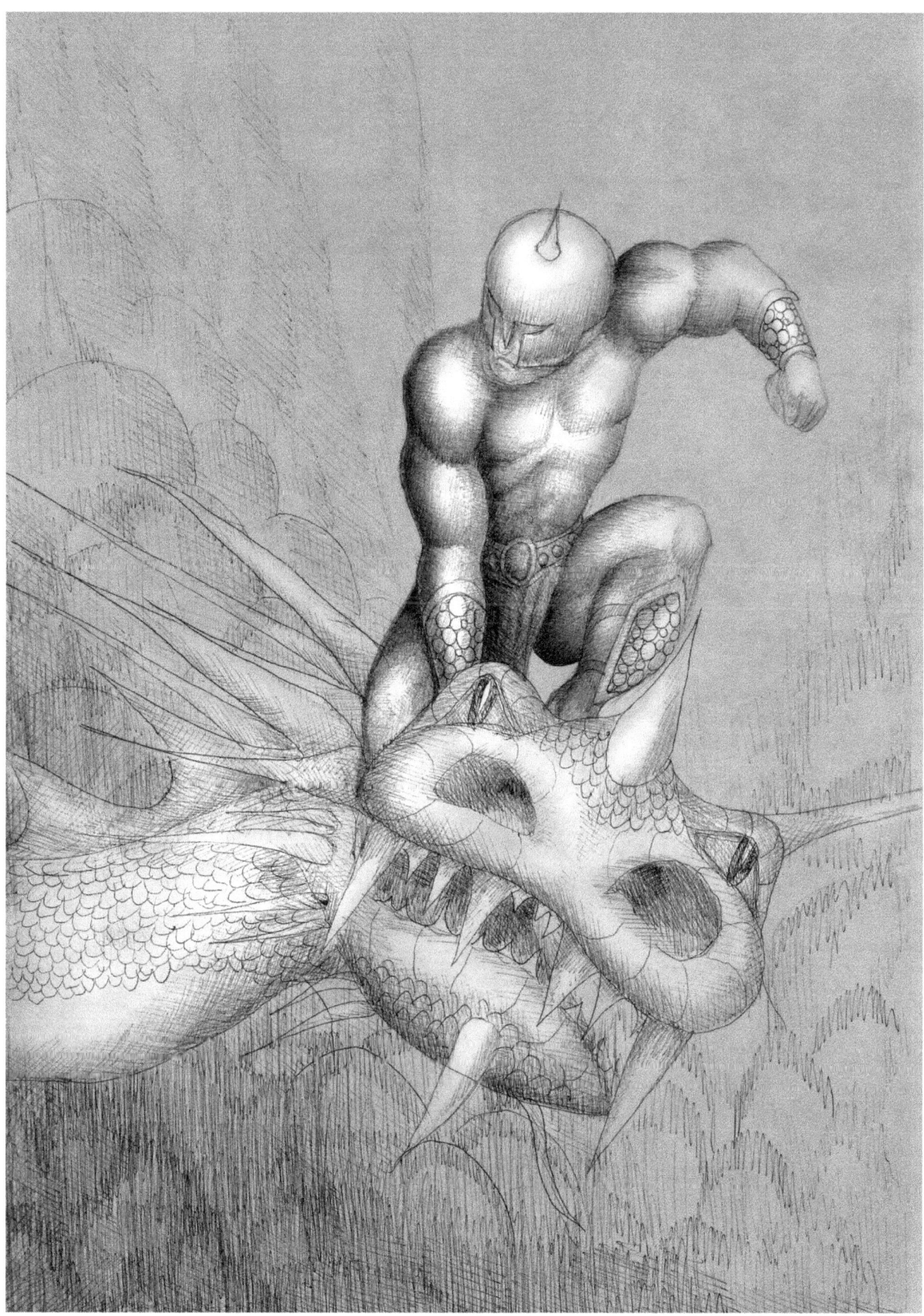

INTRODUCTION

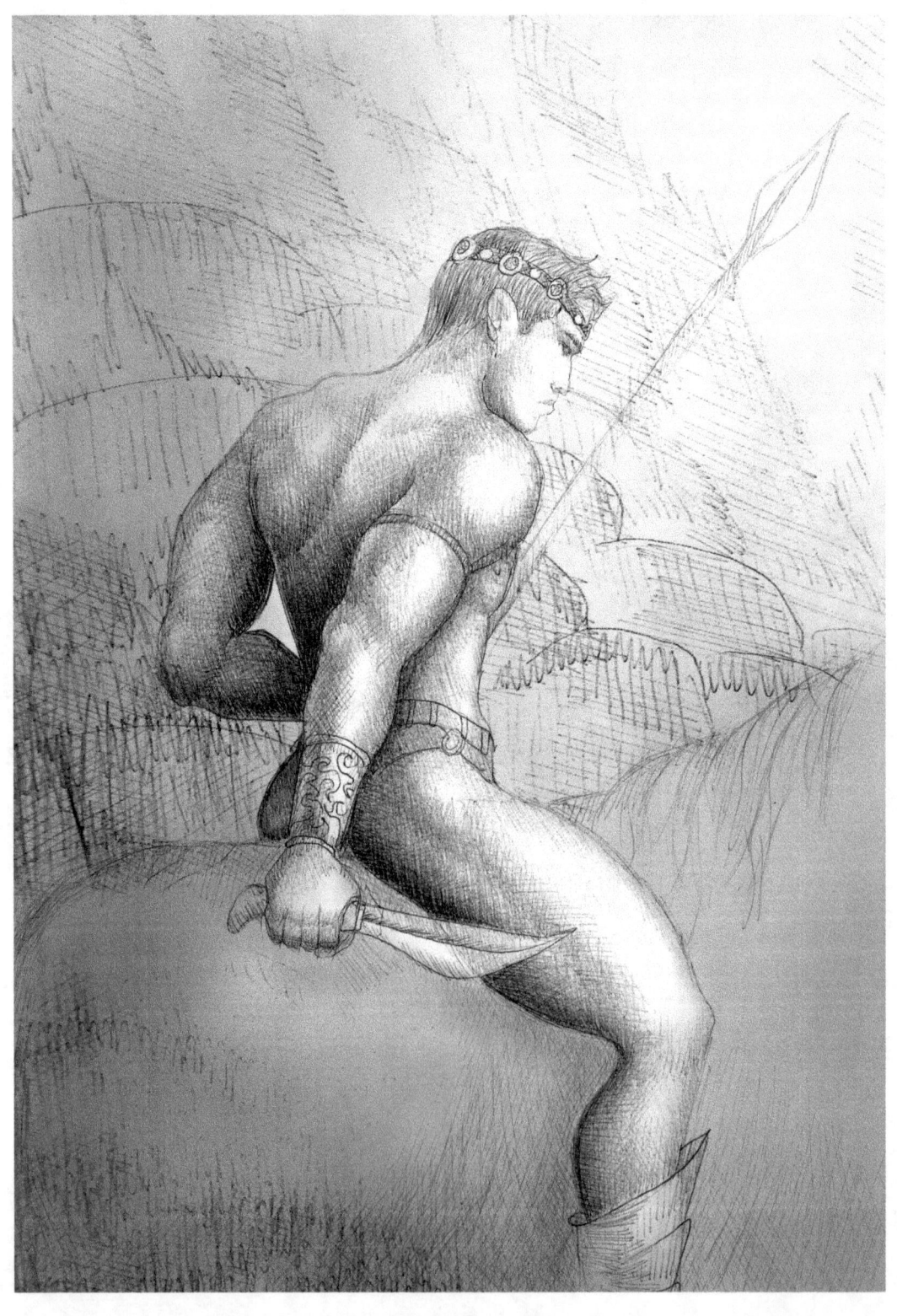

Since the beginning of mankind people have told myths and tales of the great battles and of the warriors who fought in them. Tales and legends where told of the terrible battles from Babylon to Armageddon. Battles in which thousand of warriors died and only the strongest of which survived to do battle again.

Myths and legends were spread of the terrible monsters and dragons that brave warriors would fight and slay. Such as fire breathing dragons and snakes with large fangs.

Throughout the ages there has always been a great fascination with warriors. And artists were also intrigued with the depiction of these warriors in their artwork. For example, there was Michelangelo who sculpted a powerful David against Goliath and Frank Frazetta who painted many fantasy warriors.

Artists have been inspired to paint and draw these characters larger than life. These heroes and warriors are often drawn and panted with their bodies and muscles exaggerated so as to look more fantastic and dynamic than normal. Thus inspiring the beginnings of the fantasy art genre of today.

In the fantasy art world of today artist illustrate scenes of warriors fighting, monsters and huge serpents. They fight creatures with strength and power that would instantly kill or severely hurt any normal human being. They illustrate epic battle scenes of the past and of the future.

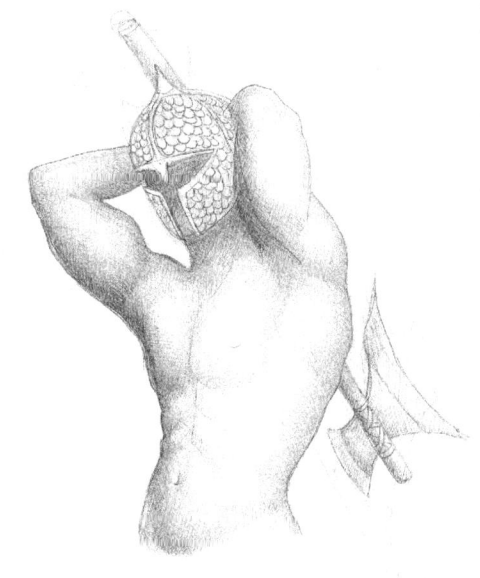

And so, it is up to you to bring your imagination to life and draw your warrior characters with artistic originality and your own style. Let the infinite reaches of your creative mind be your guide. Do not be afraid to enter the darkest realms of your imagination to find the seeds of your inspiration.

Sometimes I like to sit back and relax and just let my imagination run wild and come up with lots of ideas. I visualize just how I want each character to look like. I imagine each character has a backstory and even what type of personality they might have. I even imagine them talking to me and to each other. But mostly, I just like to have fun when I am drawing a character. So, I highly recommend that you have fun with your drawings and this in turn will show in the spirit of your artwork.

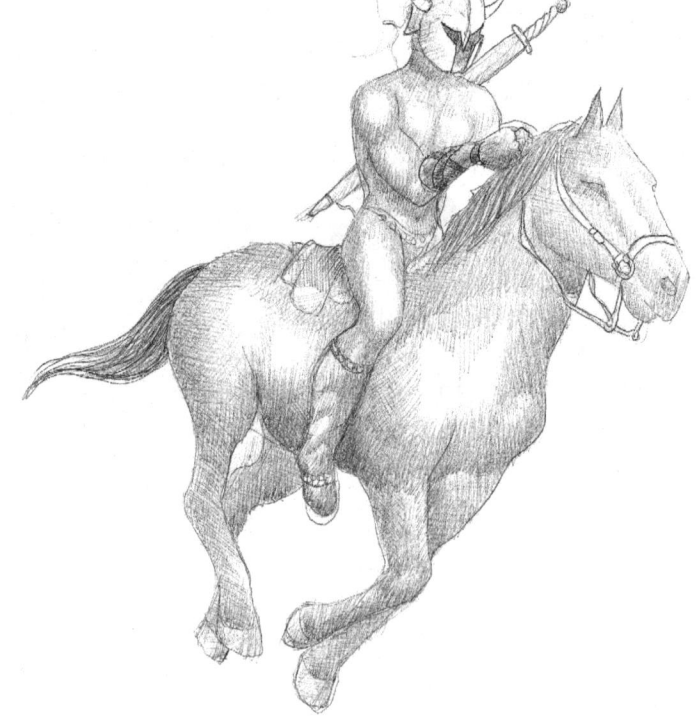

Chapter 1

Tools and Techniques
Of the Trade

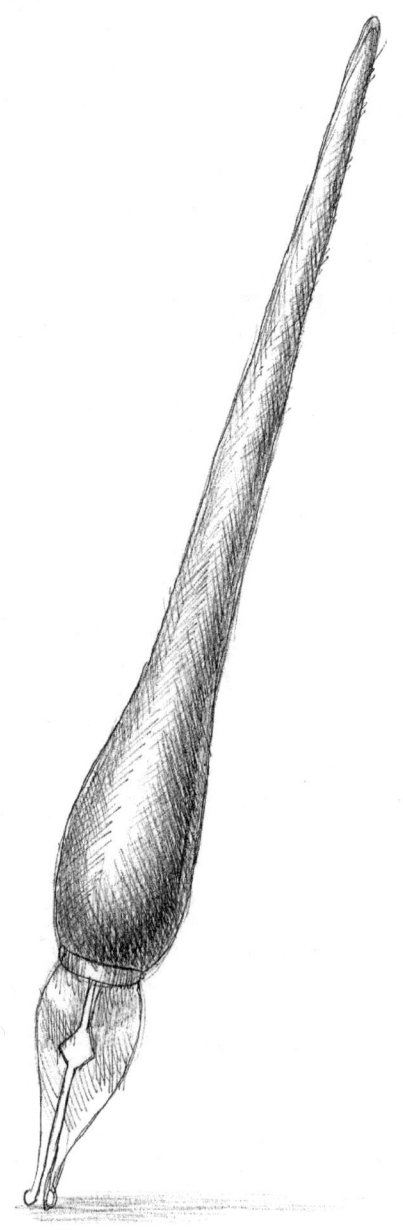

The medium and the tools that you chose are entirely up to you. I recommend that you visit your local arts supply store and just look through all the different mediums and tools that are available to you. Then try out as many of them as you can. I believe that every artist has their own special medium and tools that are just right for them. That is why it is very important not to limit or get trapped into just using one type of medium or tools. Here is a list of just a few of the mediums and tools you will find.

Drawing tools:

    Pencils
    Pen and ink
    Ball point pens
    Markers
    Conte Crayons
    Chalk
    Pastels
    Charcoals

Variety of papers:

    Drawing paper
    Poster board
    Bristol board
    Construction paper
    News print
    Butcher paper
    Canvas paper
    Parchment
    Graphic paper

By trying out and working with different art supplies you will find what works best for you.

Charcoal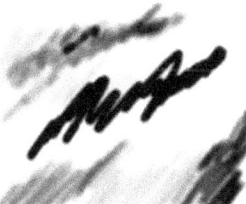

Conte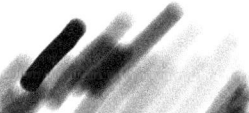

Pastel

Pen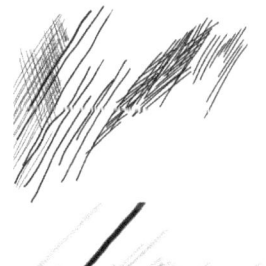

Pencil

This is just a tiny example of what is available to you. Remember it is very important to explore all of the choices of mediums.

Here are just a few examples
of techniques:

Cross Hatching: Crisp
clean lines.

Soft Blending: Smooth
shading

Coarse Blending:
Dark strong blending

Ink Wash: Deep and
soft shading

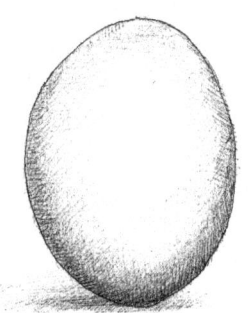

CROSS HATCH
TECHNIQUE

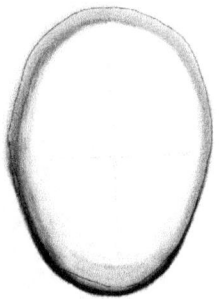

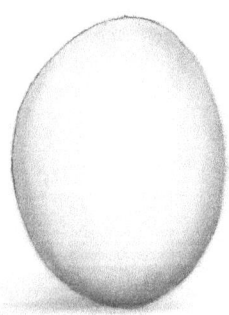

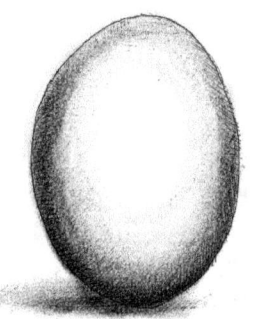

INK WASH
TECHNIQUE

SOFT
BLENDING
TECHNIQUE

CHARCOAL
TECHNIQUE

- It is a good idea to practice drawing and shading basic shapes, such as circles, squares, triangles, ovals and tubular objects.

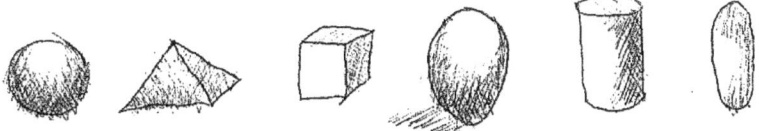

- These are just a few of the basic shapes that make up everyday objects.

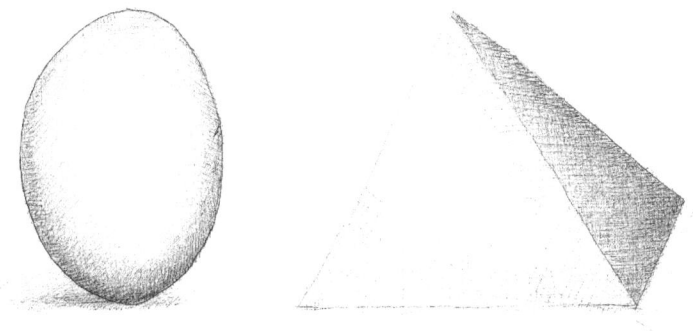

- Practice your shading technique using a bar scale drawing, going from dark to light.

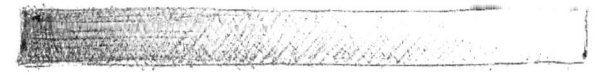

9

As the artist, it is up to you to explore the creative essence of your own mind. It is the work of the artist to give all the ideas and emotions inside the mind a physical form.

It is through the expression and embodiment of these thoughts that art is created. Therefor, the mind is one of the greatest tools of an artist. Like any tool or technique the mind must be trained and developed. Then it can function with the hand to create and present art.

Through deep meditation and concentration exercises your mind can learn to enter into the creative realm. It is a place where you will find a source of highly creative energy. There is a universe of creative ideas inside the mind of every artist and it's up to you to explore it.

True art is the ability to express your soul on the canvas and that is what makes a true artist. When someone can see beyond what you create and actually understand it then it is like touching their soul.

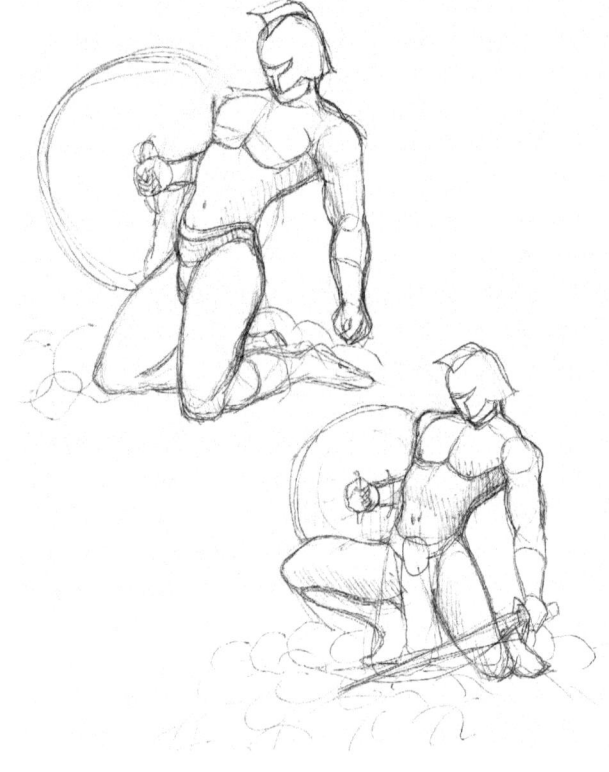

Chapter 2

Basic Anatomy

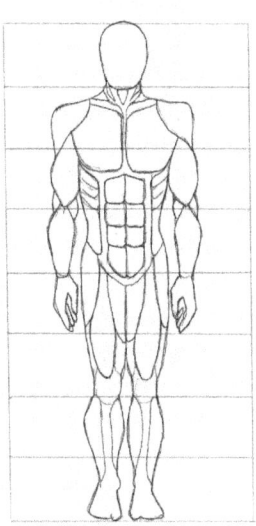

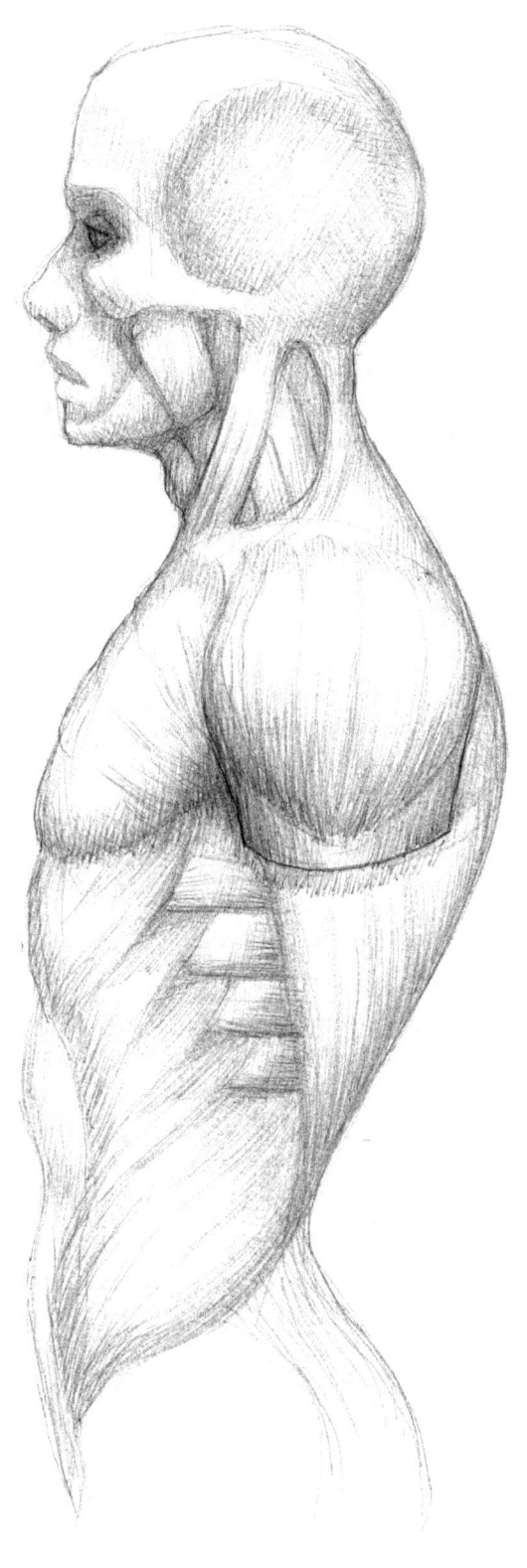

The anatomy in this book is very basic and is only for the purpose of having a fundamental understanding as it relates to the artist. I have simplified the muscle charts to show the basic muscle groups of the human body. This will give you a basic understanding of how the muscle groups appear in the body. As a beginning artist I feel that you shouldn't become preoccupied with knowing every single muscle and its name. Therefor, the charts in this book have been simplified to give an uncomplicated approach to drawing a muscular figure.

Practice drawing the charts of the figures.

Divide each chart into eight sections tall each section roughly equal to eight heads

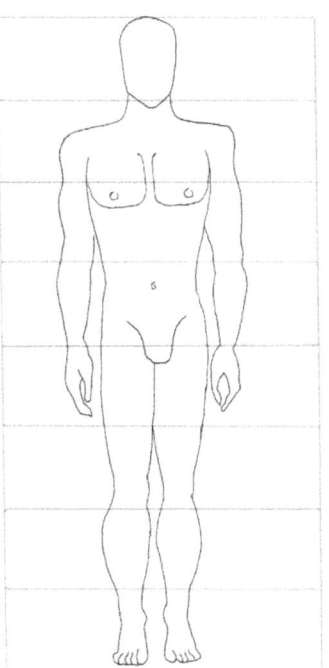

- Draw the upper body including the head in the in the upper four sections.
- Draw the arms slightly below the second section, which will make them slightly less than four sections in length.
- Draw the legs and the feet in the lower four sections.

BASIC SKELETAL FRONT VIEW:

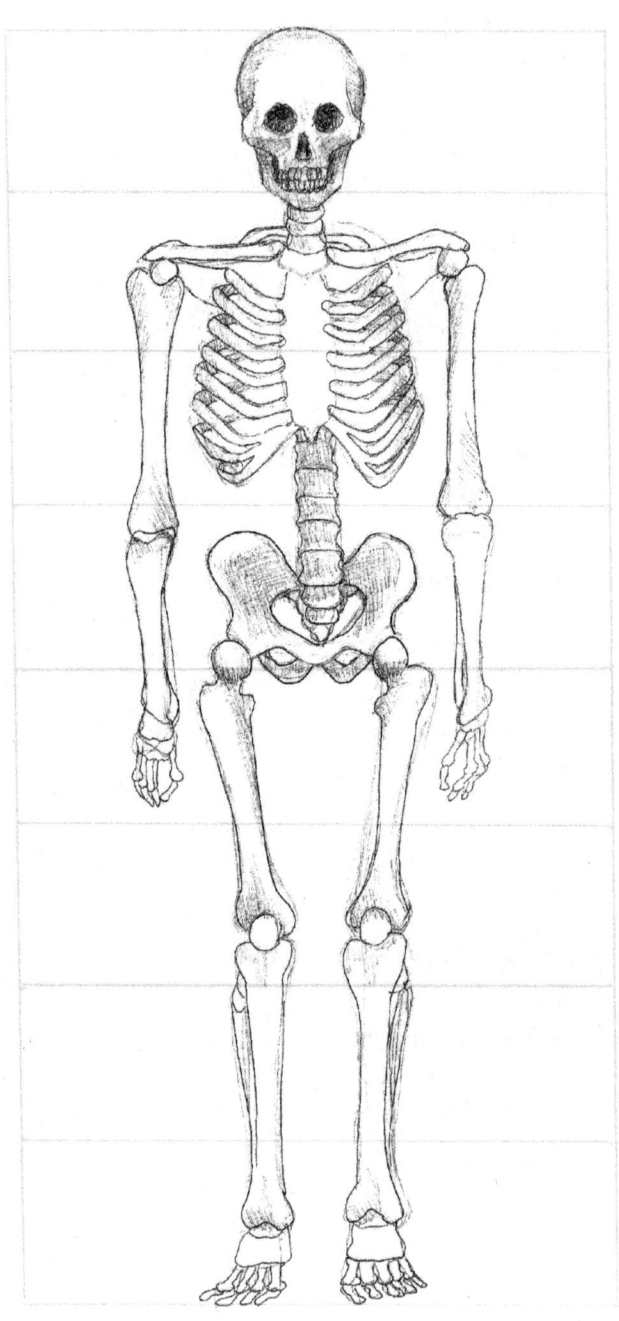

BASIC SHAPES IN THE BODY

These are the basic shapes that compose the figure.

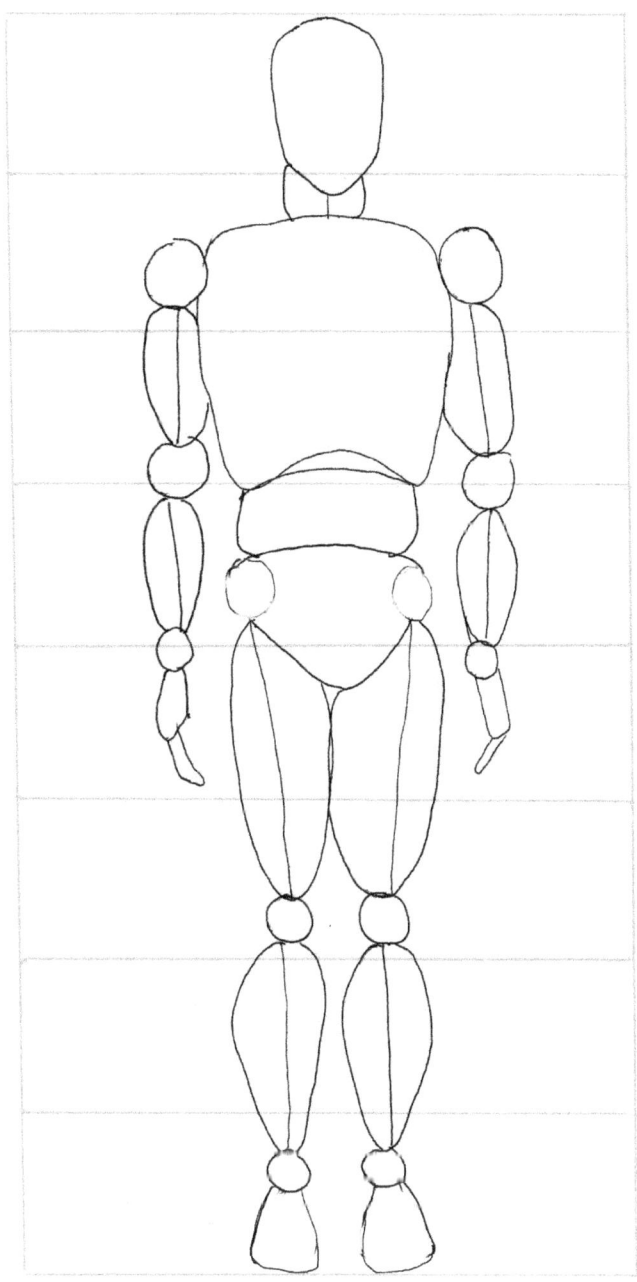

BASIC MUSCLE SHAPES

This is the front view of the basic muscle groups of the male body.

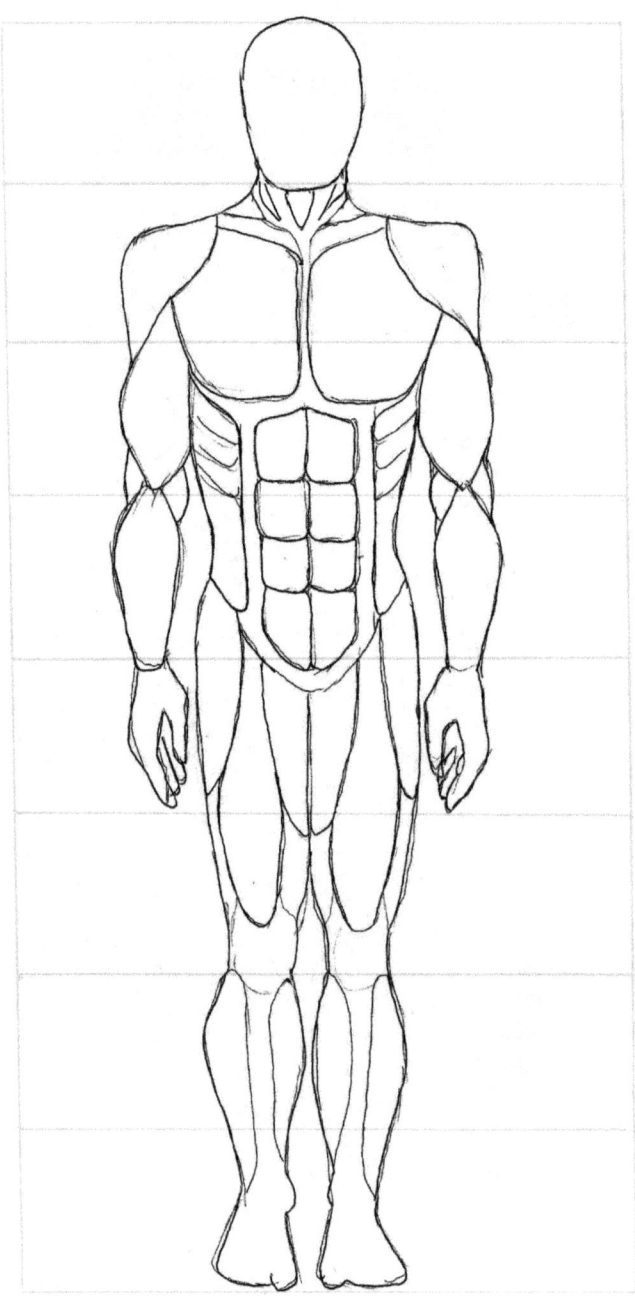

BASIC MUSCLE SHAPES

This is the backside view of the basic muscle groups in the male body.

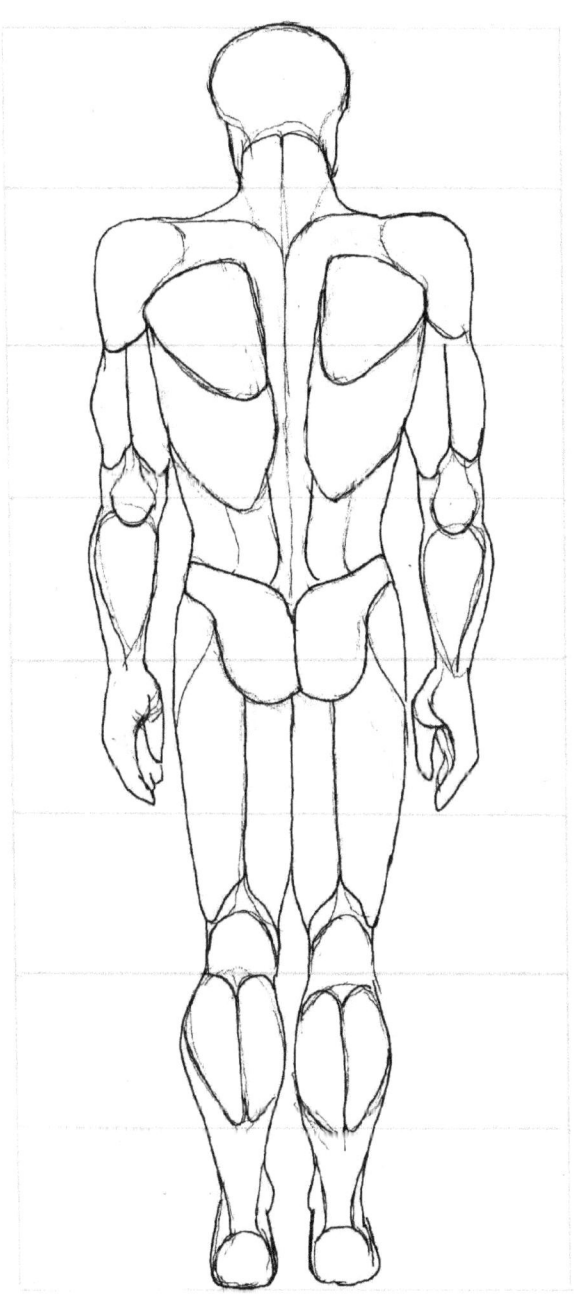

BASIC MUSCLE SHAPES

This is the side view of the basic muscle groups.

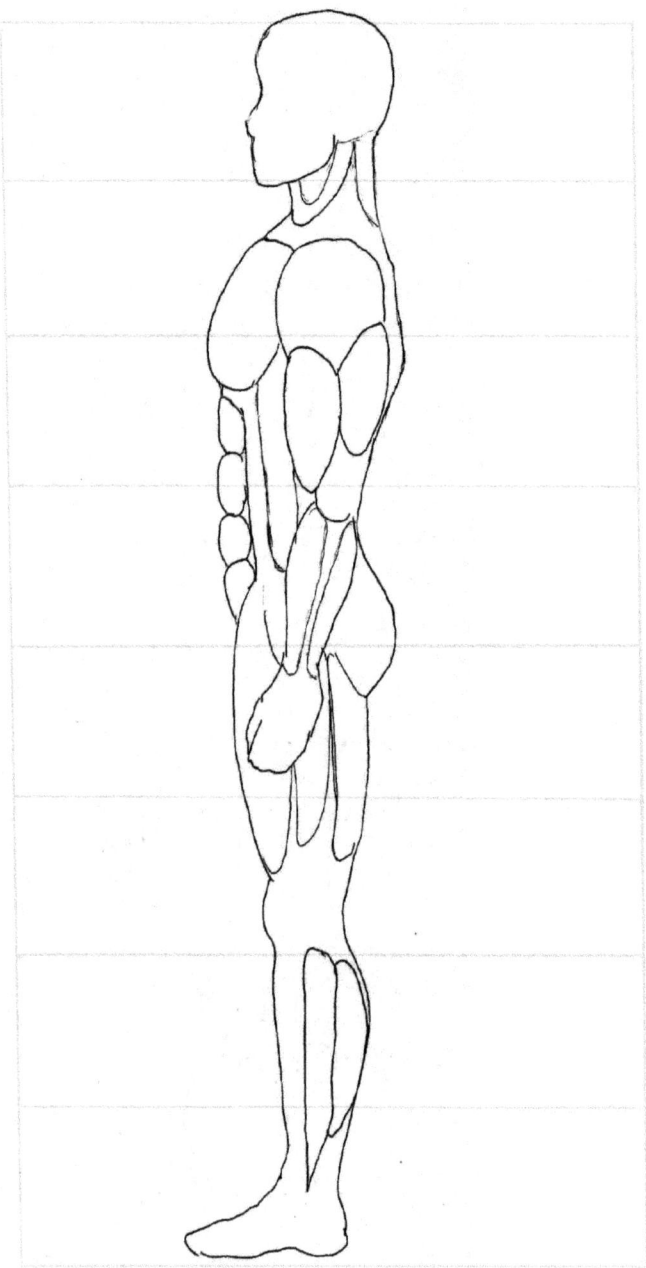

8 section body scale chart.

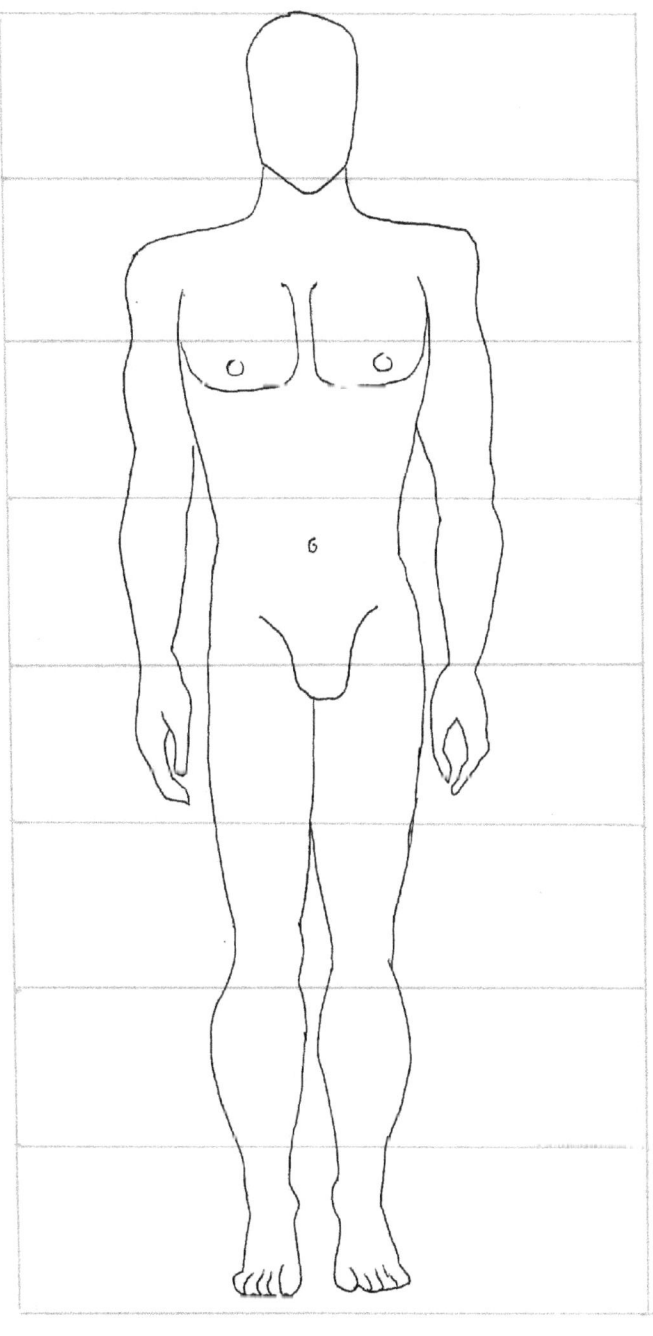

Chapter 3

Drawing the body

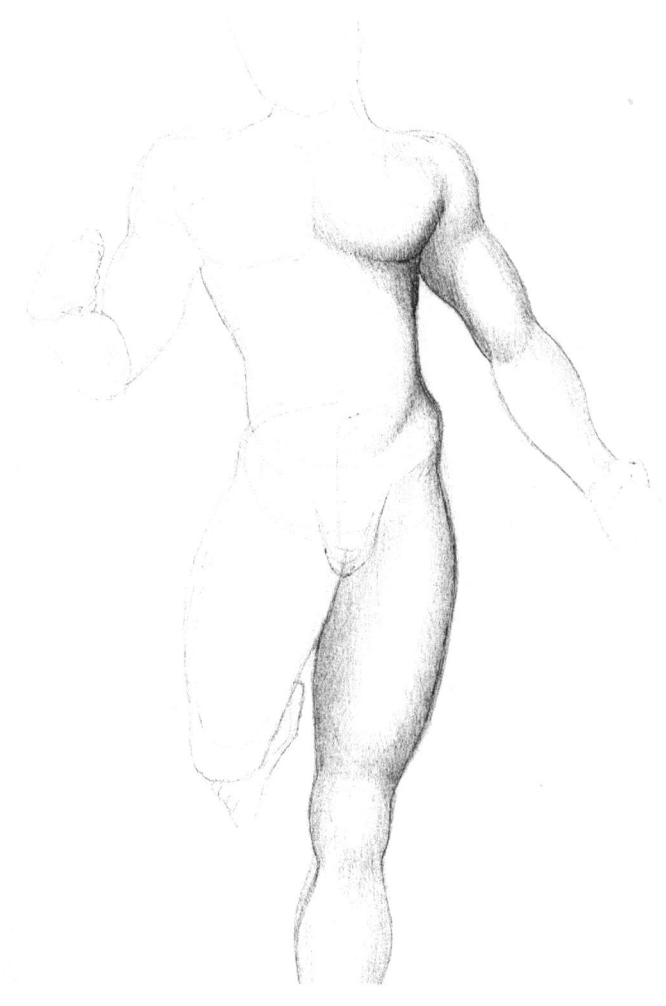

Drawing the torso

 Select the pose or position you want for the figure.

 Begin drawing the torso using circular shapes then outline the shapes.

Figure: 1 and 2

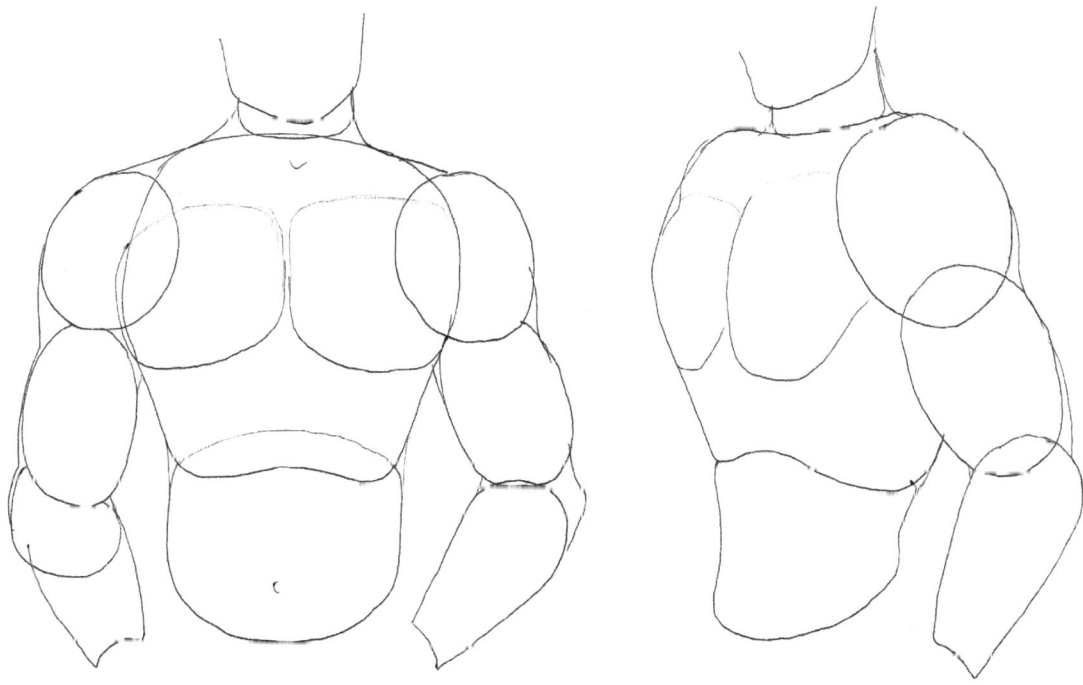

Now, you can outline the shapes.
In this stage you should add all the
extra details to the torso. Define
the chest area and the abdominal
areas.

Figure: 3 and 4

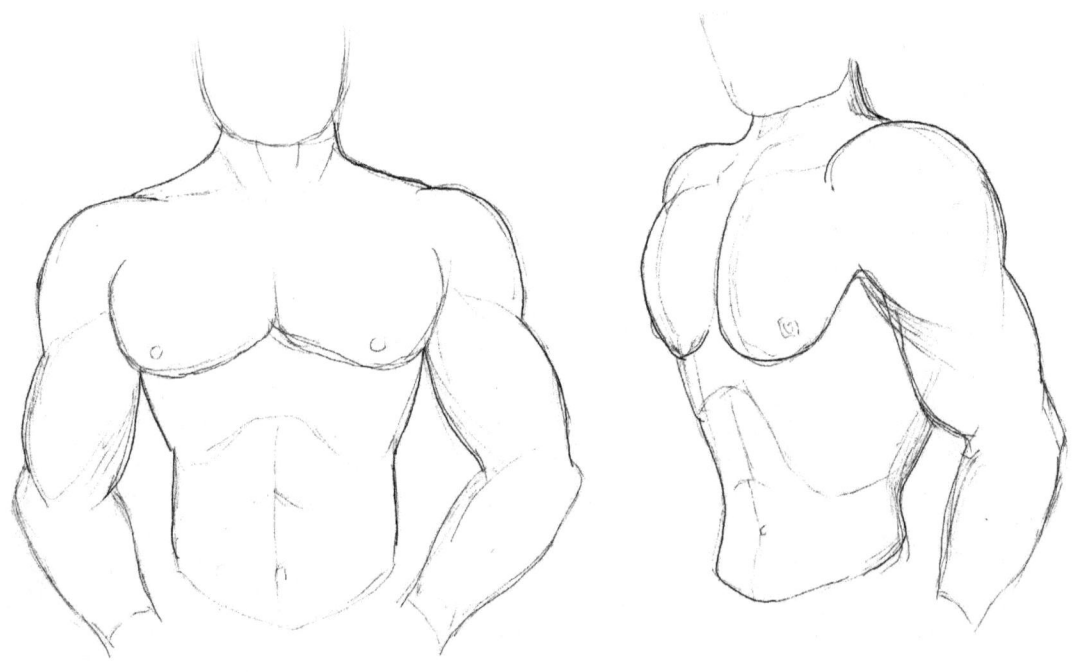

 In the following steps you can start to slowly shade in the torso.
Work slowly and delicately as you shade in the contours of the torso.
When you have shaded the overall torso, go back and darken the
deep shadows.

Figure: 5 and 6

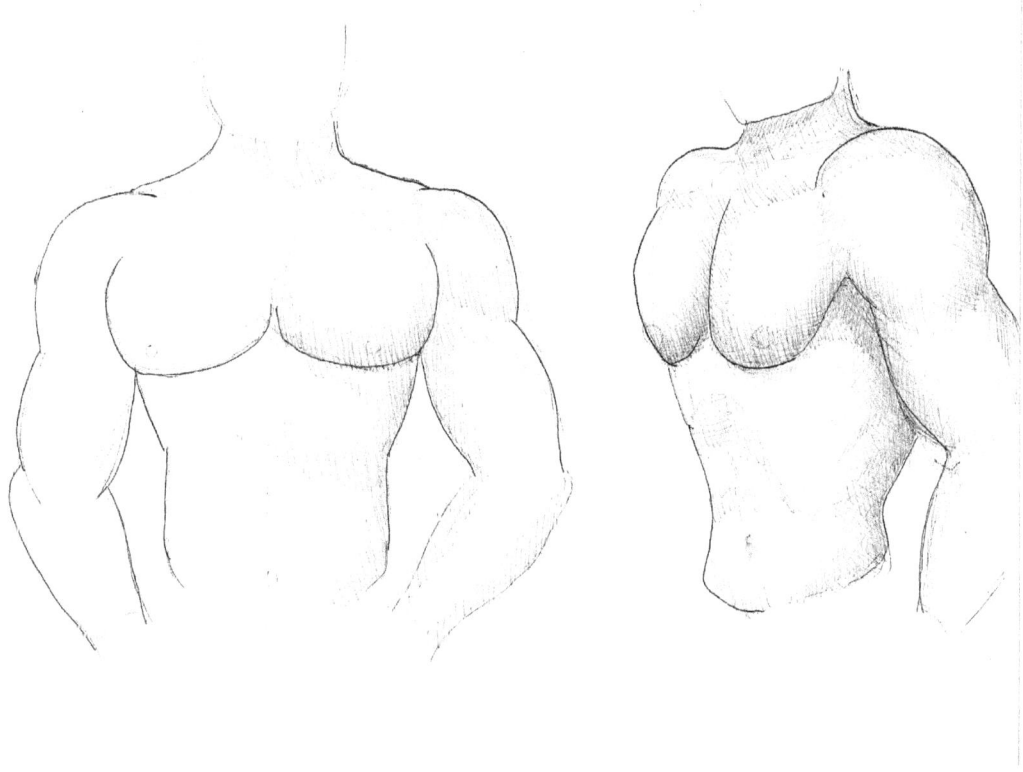

Figure: 7 and 8

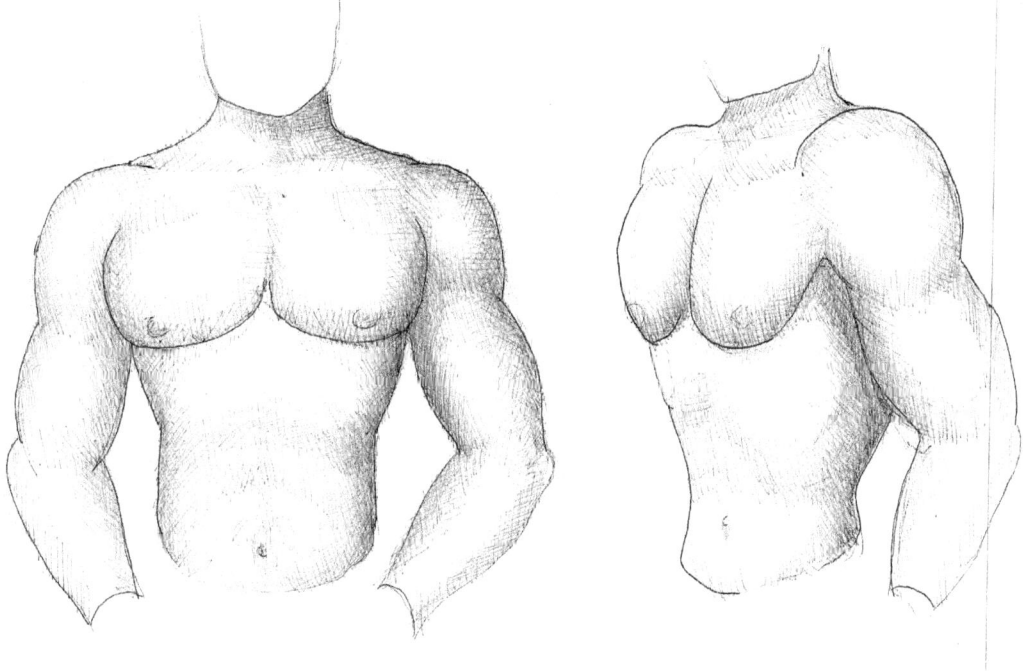

Drawing the arms

Begin by drawing circular shapes
to from the arms.

Outline the shapes and circles to
form the arm.

Figure: 1

Figure: 2

Figure: 3

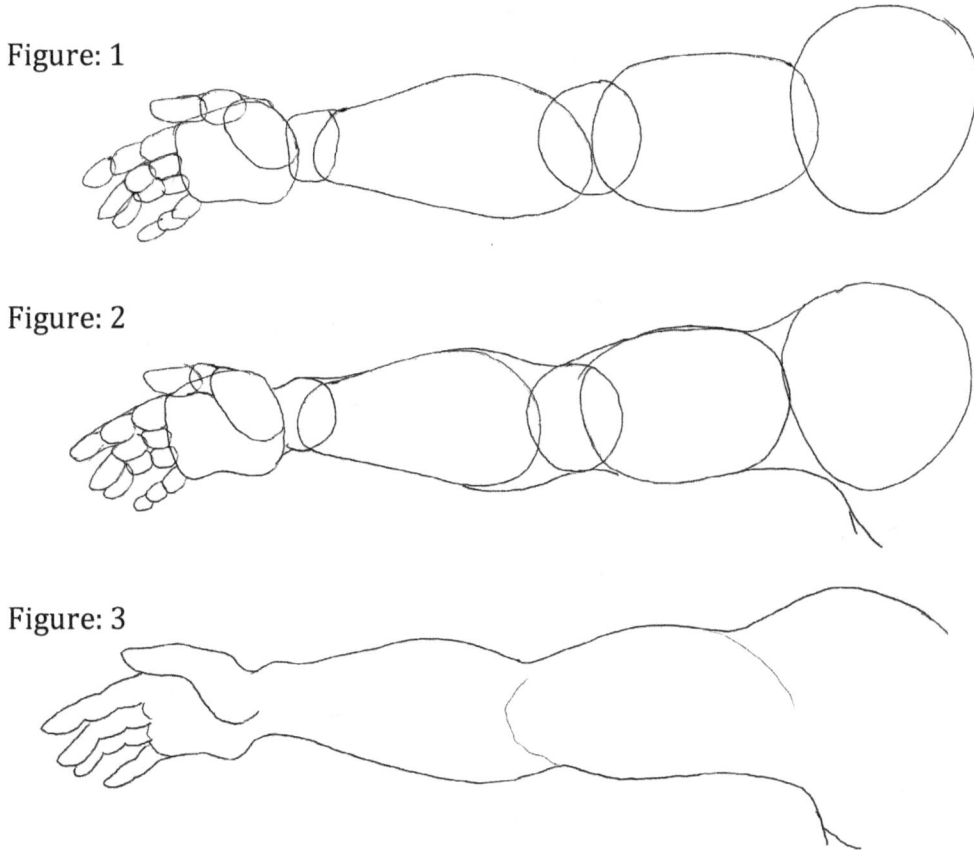

Once you have completed the outline drawing you are now ready to begin shading the muscle area.

Determine where the angle of the light is coming from then begin to shade in the area.

Shade in the entire area that is in shade. Next, add detail shading to the individual muscle. You can work from light to dark or the opposite.

Figure: 4

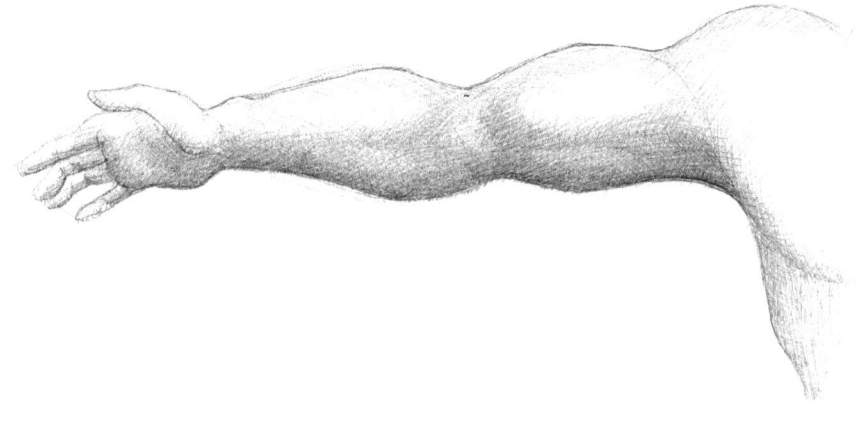

35

Drawing the legs

Front view:
Start by drawing the oblong
shapes first.

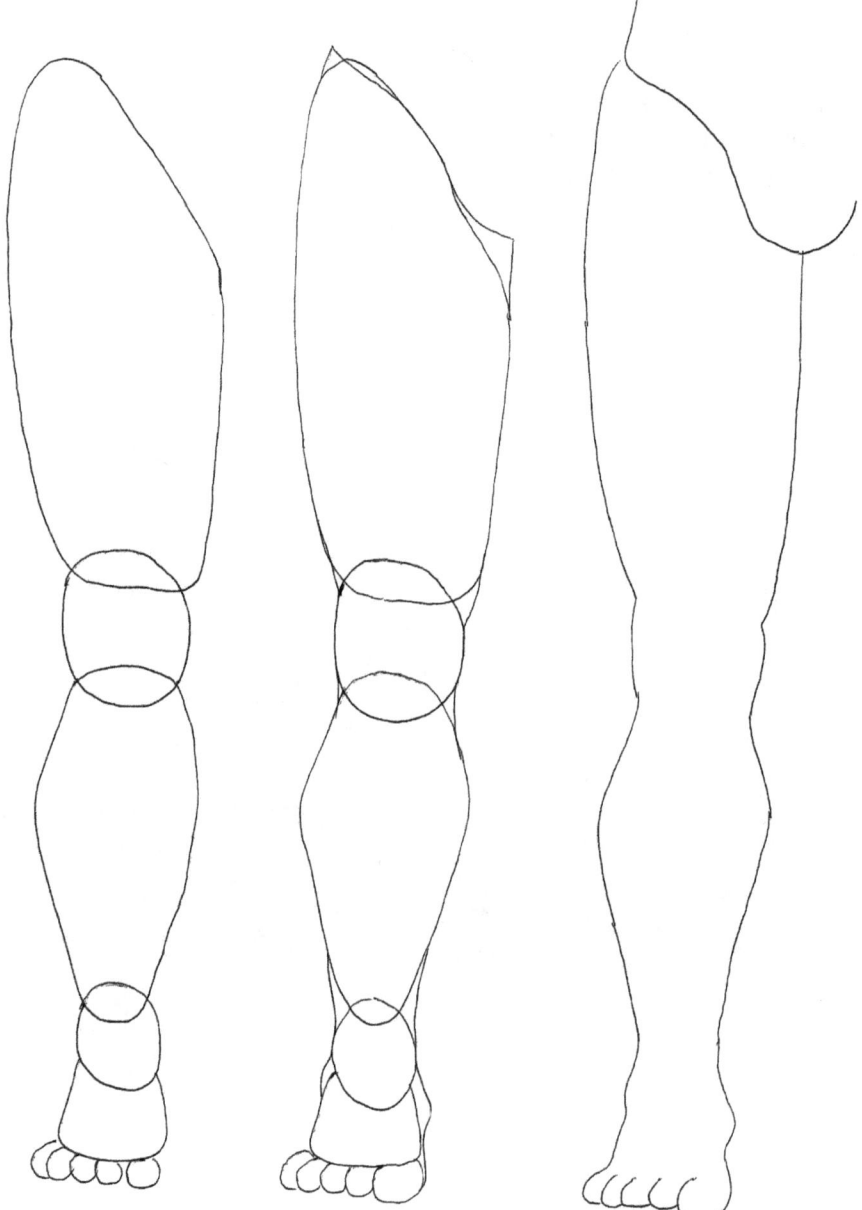

Figures: 1, 2, 3

Figure: 4

The darker the shading, the more it will make the muscles standout.

Figure: 5

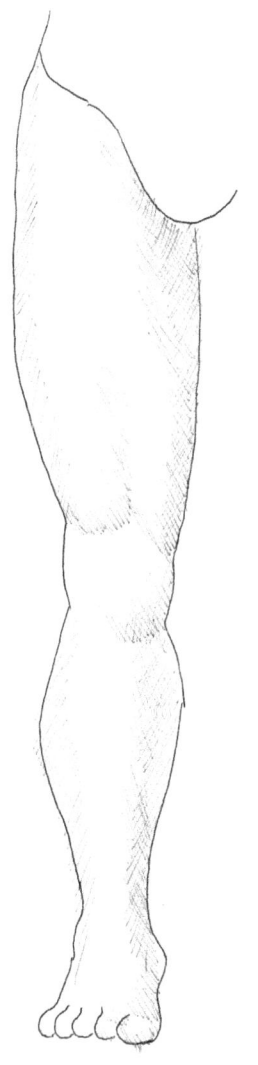

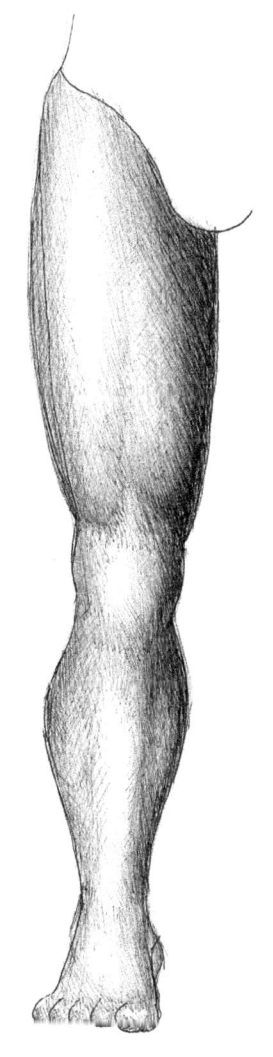

Start to shade the largest muscle mass first. Then work on the smaller areas next.

Side view

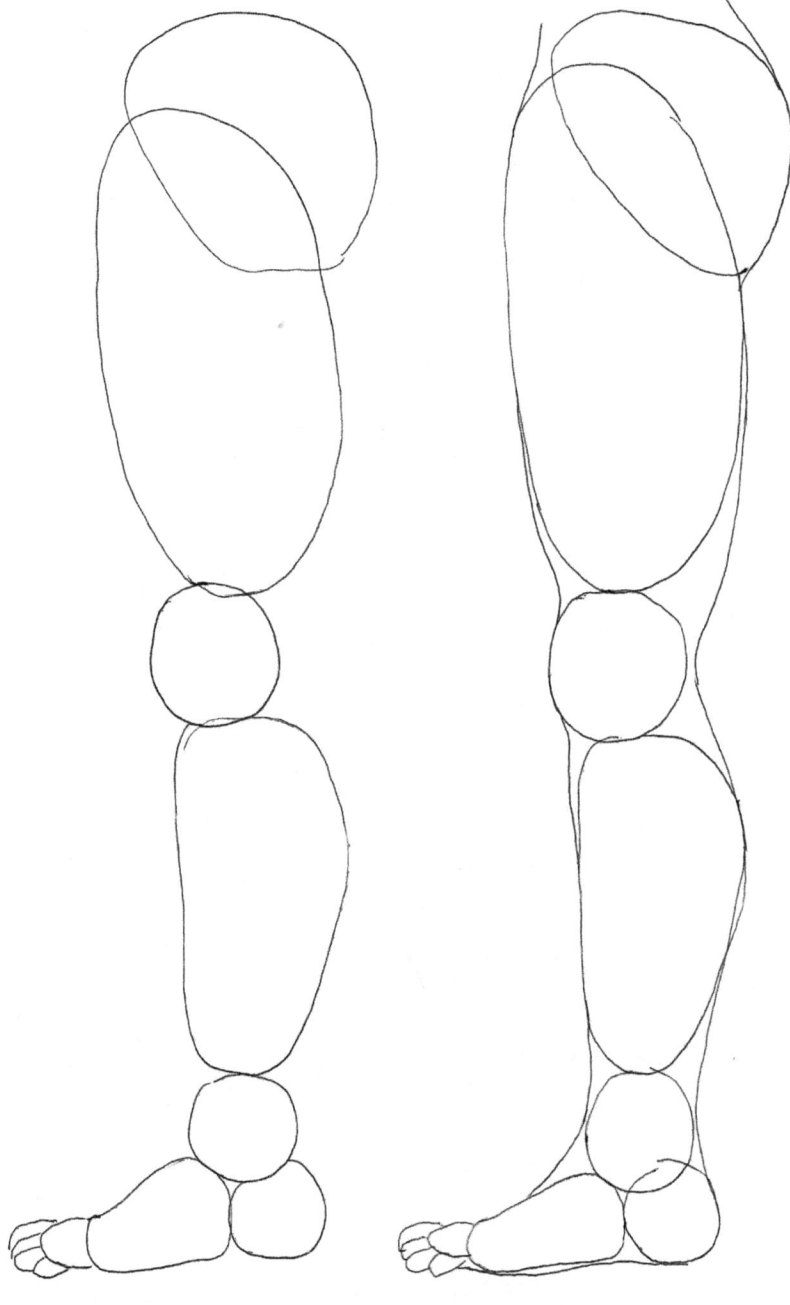

Figure: 1   Figure: 2

Once you have the outline shade
in the large muscle groups.

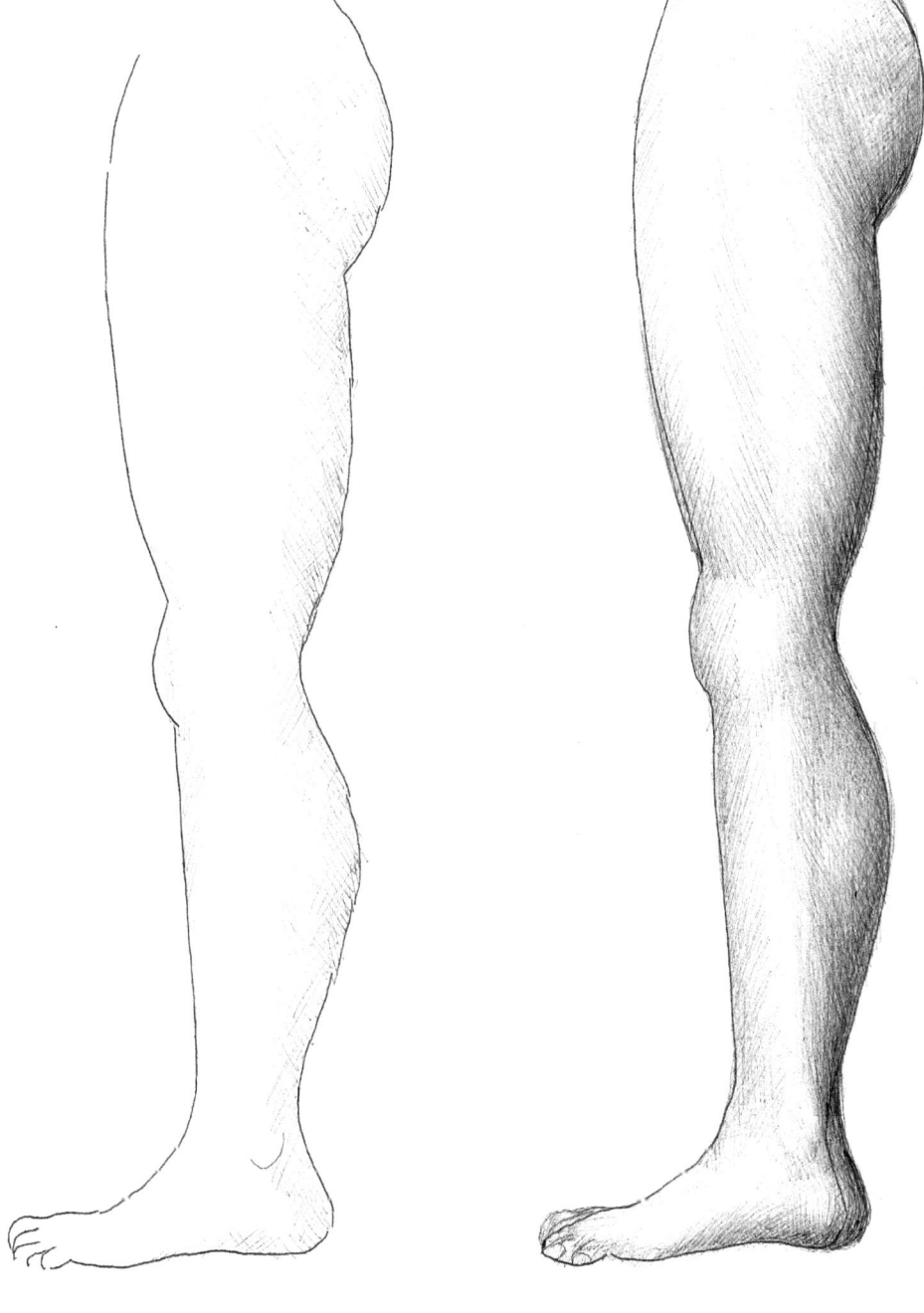

Figure: 3   Figure: 4

Drawing hands

When drawing the hands you must be meticulous about drawing all the shapes that are found in its composition. Outline the entire shape to from the hand.

Figure group: 1, 2, 3

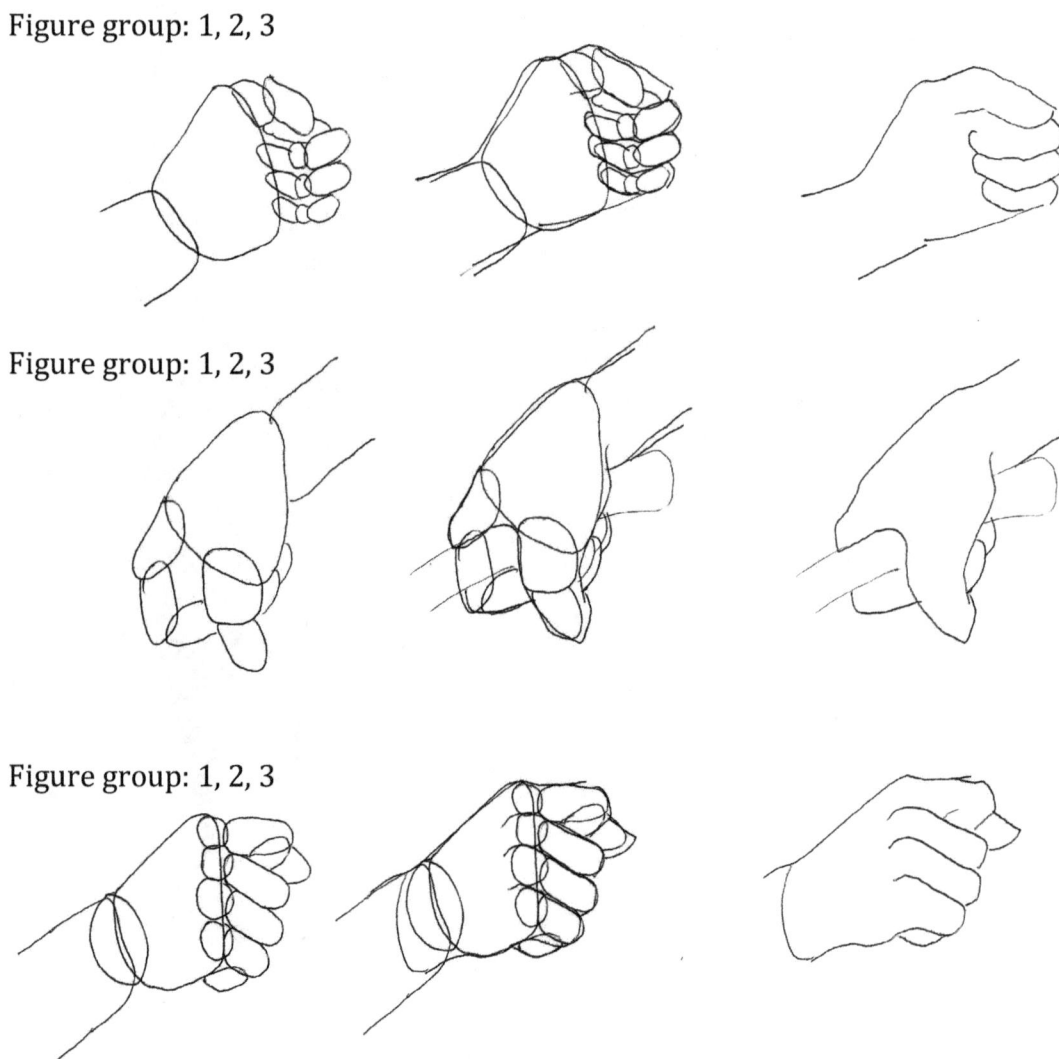

Figure group: 1, 2, 3

Figure group: 1, 2, 3

Be meticulous about shading in all the areas of the hand. There is a lot of detail shading that must be done when drawing the hands. Take your time when shading in the hands.

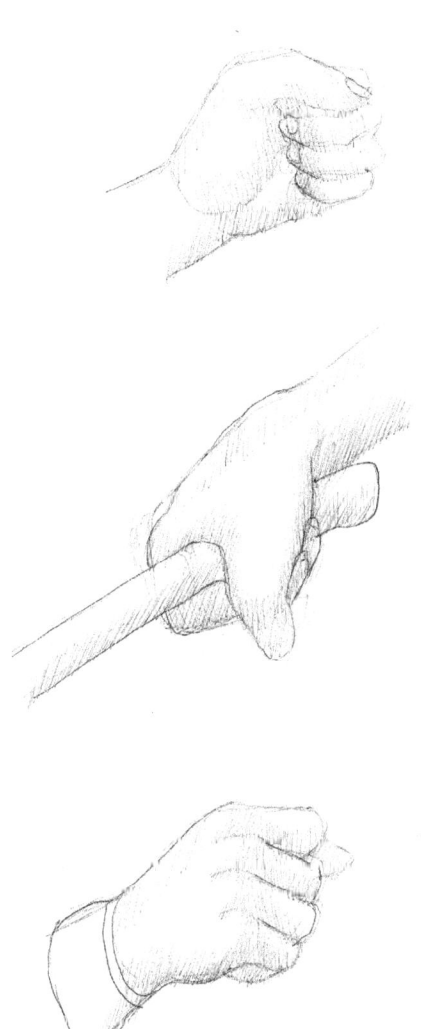

Drawing the feet

Figure group: 1, 2, 3

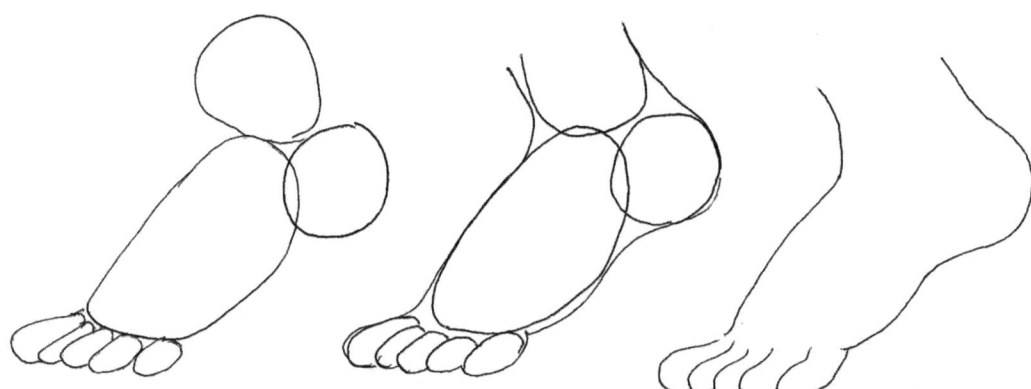

Figure group: 1, 2, 3

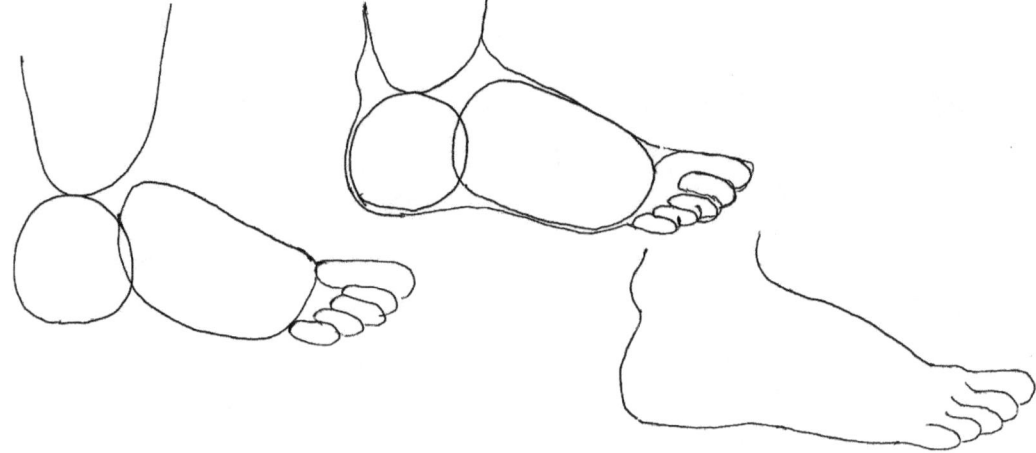

The feet have a lot of small components that make up the entire foot. Be meticulous and precise when shading in everything.

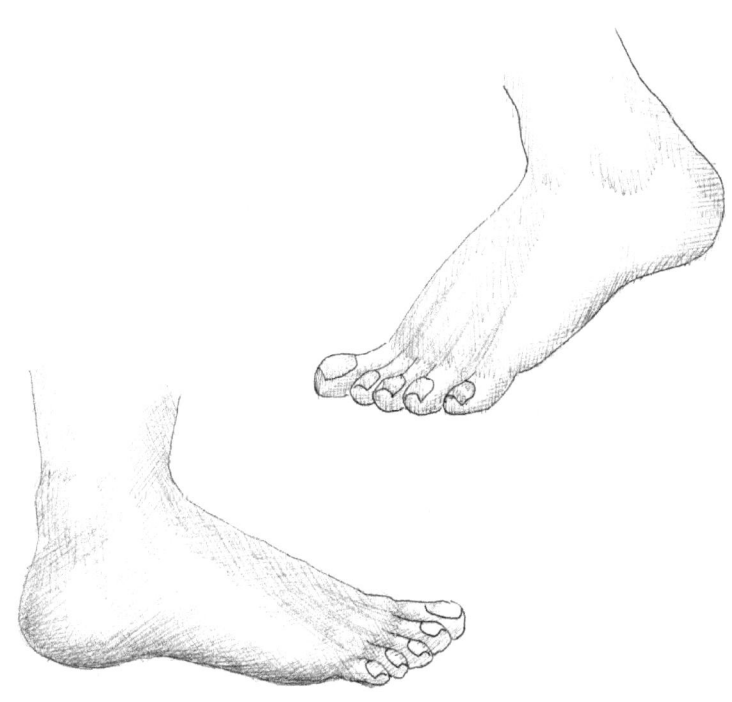

Chapter 4

Drawing the head and face

Practice drawing the skull
as delicately and lightly as
you can. Then practice
drawing ovals and circles for
the shape of the head and
face.

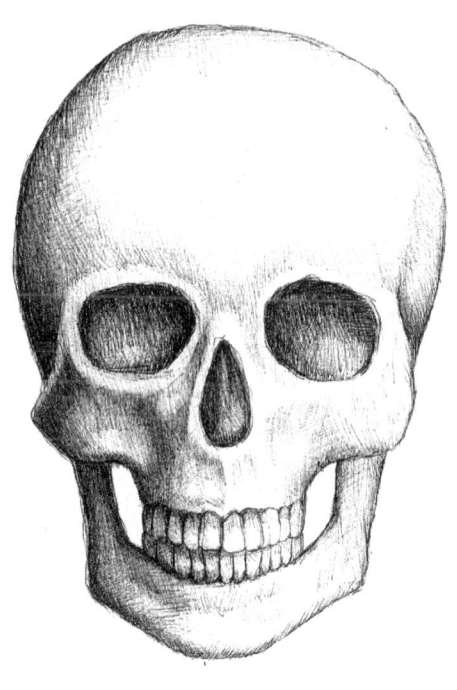

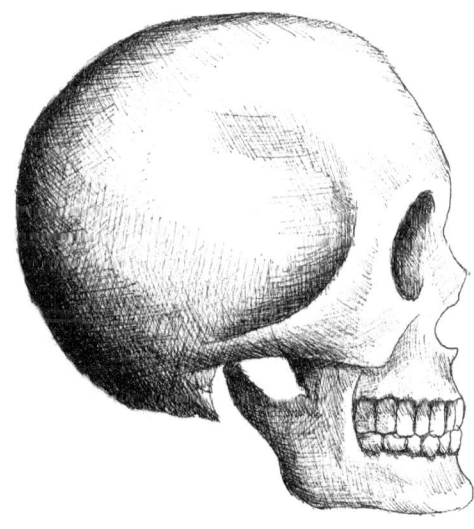

Figure: 1

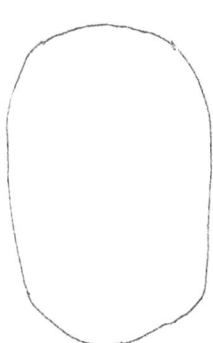

Figure: 2

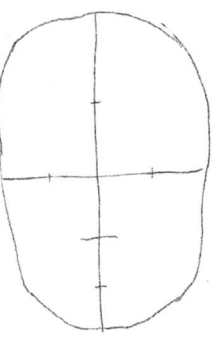

First draw an oval
Then divide it into four parts.

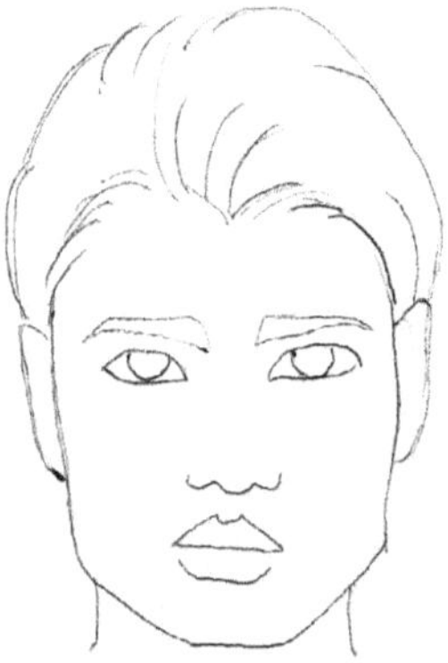

The middle horizontal line will
serve as the eye placement guide.

The centerline is the nose guide.

Divide the lower half of the oval for
the bottom of the nose mark.

Place the lip guide directly between
the bottom nose mark and the
bottom of the oval.

Now you can draw in the face
features.

Draw in all the details like the
eyebrows and hair.

Establish the light direction and
begin to shade the face.

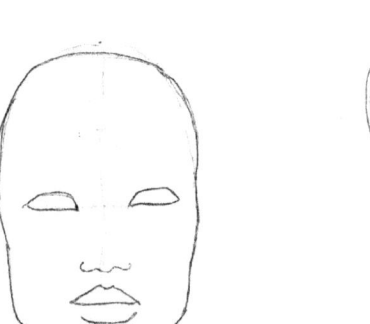

Figure: 3

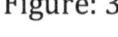

Figure: 4

Figure: 5

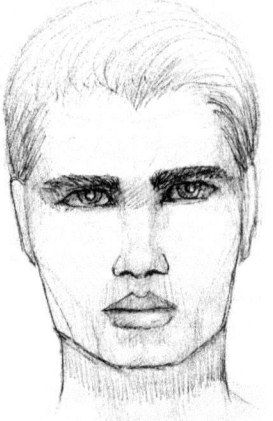

The quarter profile of the face.

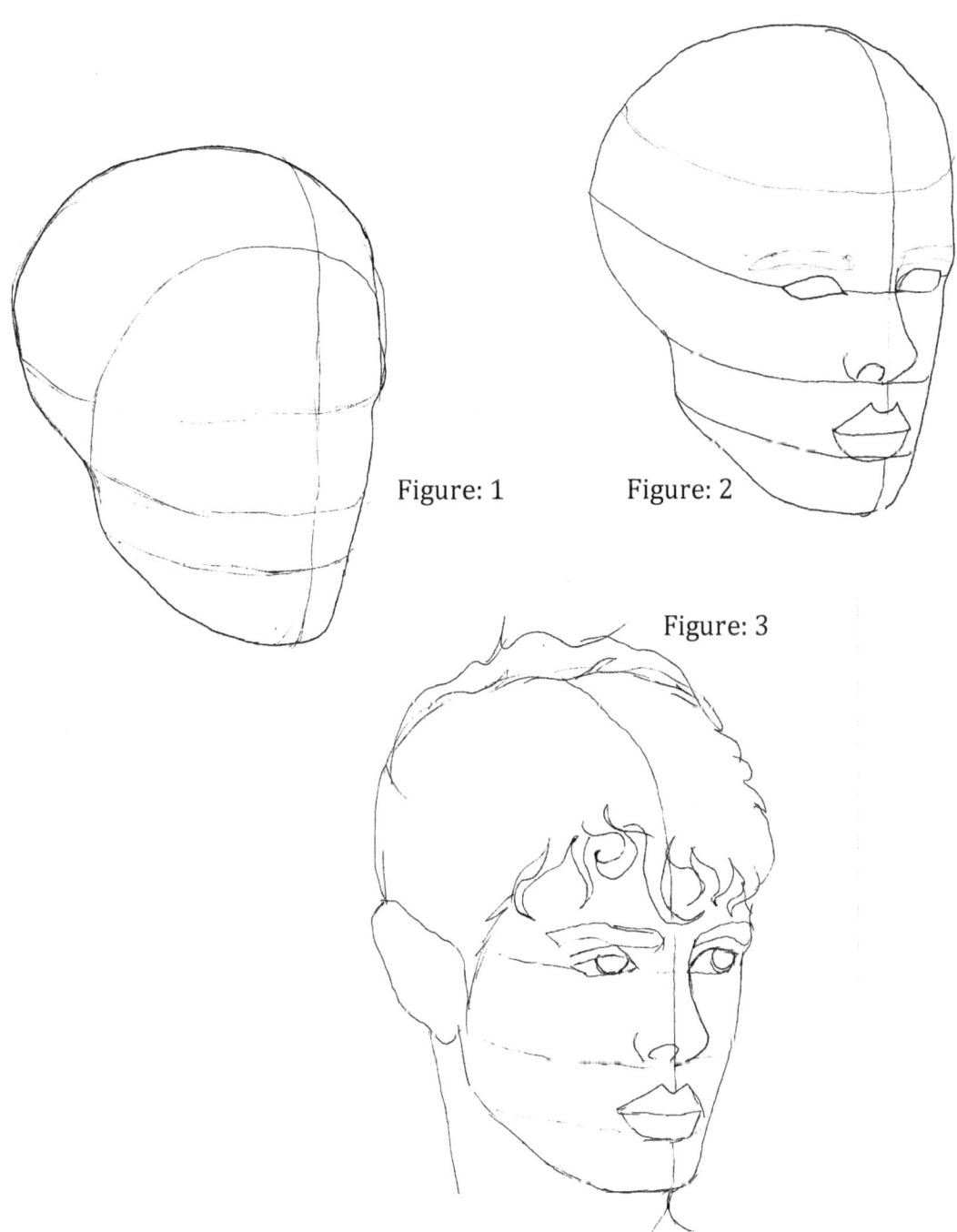

Figure: 1

Figure: 2

Figure: 3

Establish the light direction then
begin to shade the face.

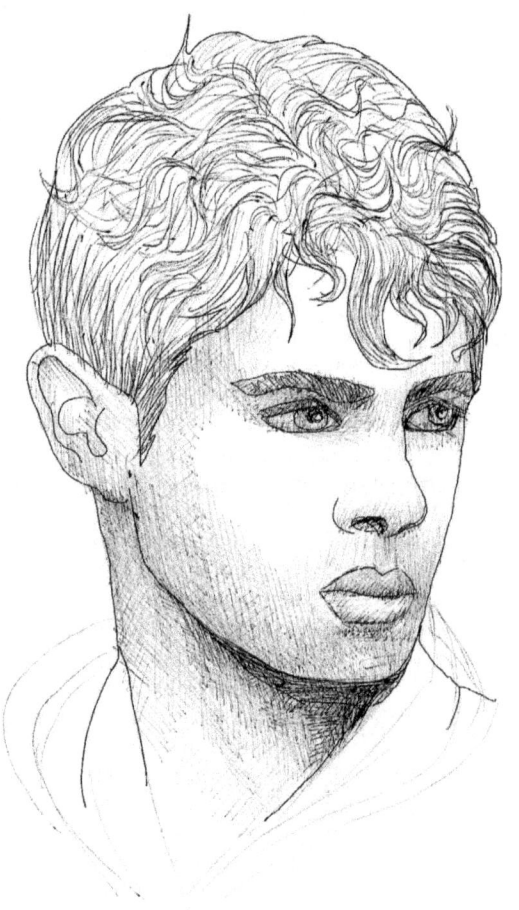

Figure: 4

The full profile of the face.

Figure: 1

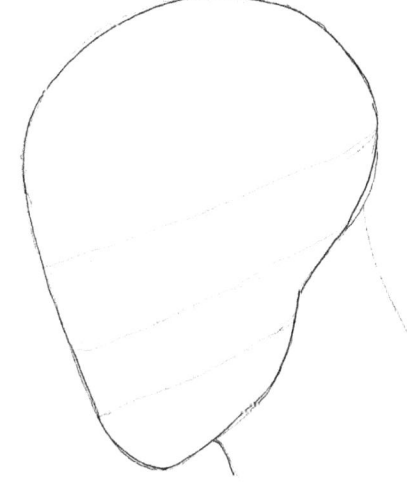

Figure: 3

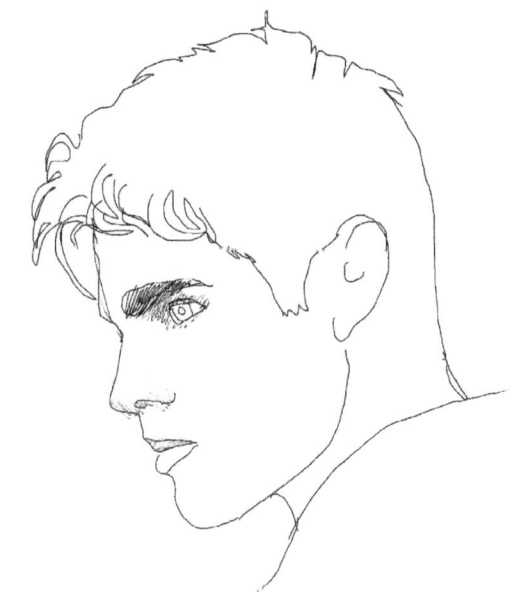

Figure: 2

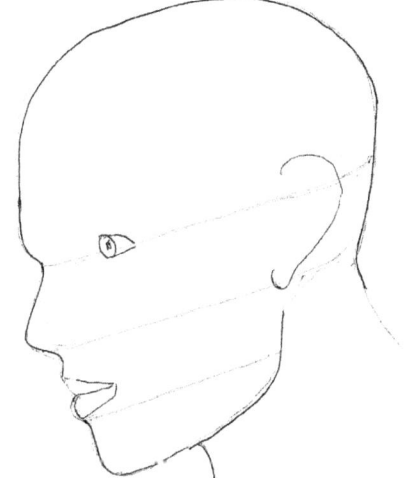

Figure: 4

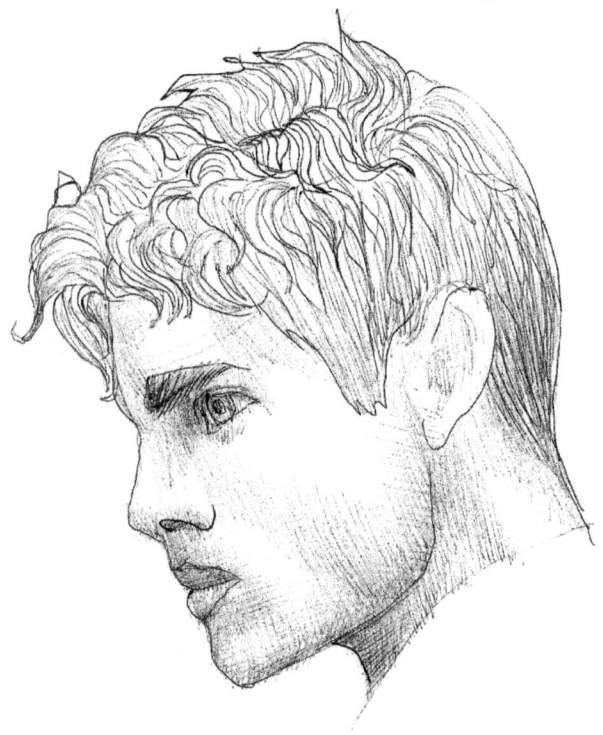

Remember that the face has a lot
of complex detail and you may
want to study it more closely.

Chapter 5

Shading process

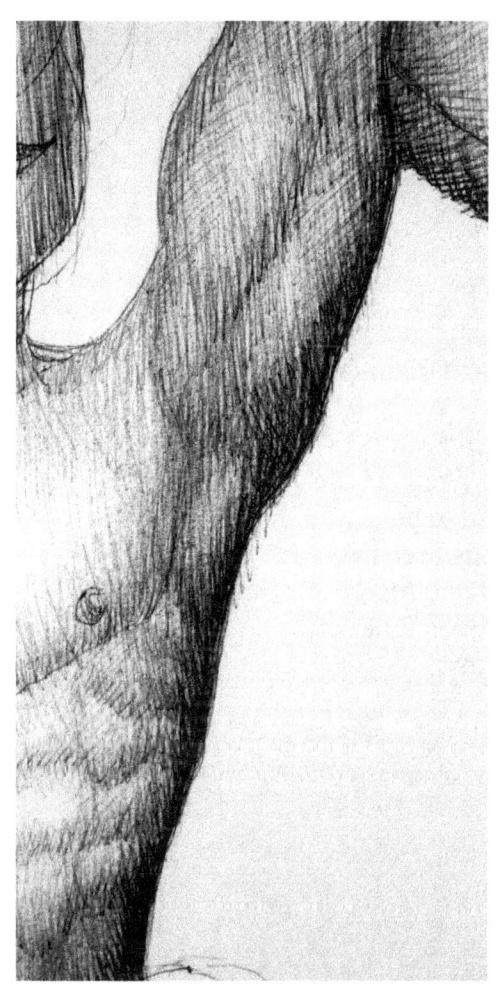

The final stage in drawing is shading everything in. At this stage make sure your drawing is just the way that you want it to be. If you can make any corrections or adjustments, do them now. Then determine the direction of the light source, and start the shading process.

- Start the shading with a general shading of the entire drawing. Lightly shade all the areas that you will be working on.
- Secondly, concentrate on the darker areas of the drawing. These are the parts of the drawing that you want to have some depth.
- Now, you can work on the specific areas of the drawing. Concentrate your shading on the individual face features.
- Lastly, go in and refine your shading. Work on the parts that need to be defined, and the areas you want to stand out. Also, work on the areas that you want the darkest.

Take as much time as you want when you are in the shading stage of your drawing. Be careful not to over shade everything. After each stage of the shading sit back, and examine your progress. Before continuing assess what areas require more work, and what areas do not. This is the final stage of your drawing, give it all that you have.

Also, it is important to note that this process does not have to be followed in the order that it is listed. For example, the detail shading can be done first.

Example One

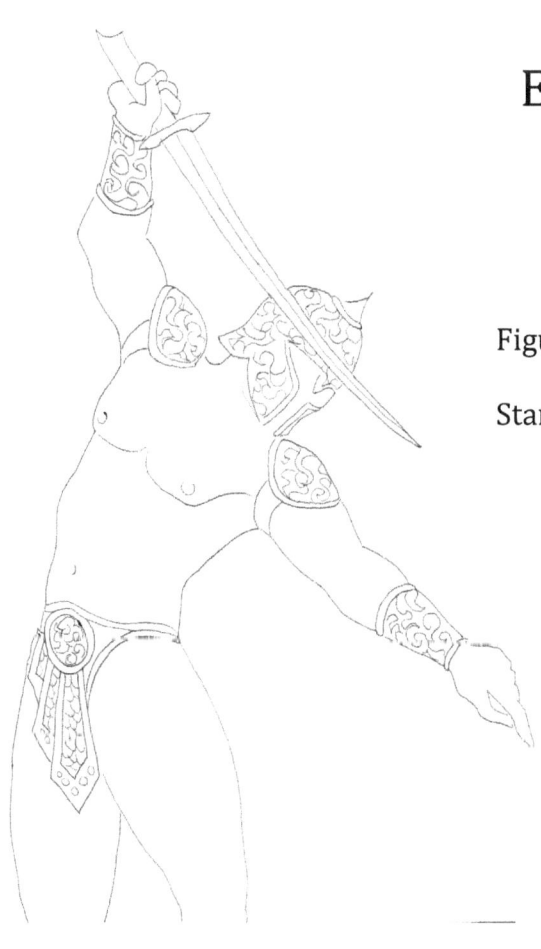

Figure: 1

Start with a good outline of the figure.

Figure: 2

Do an overall light shading of all the main areas of the figure.

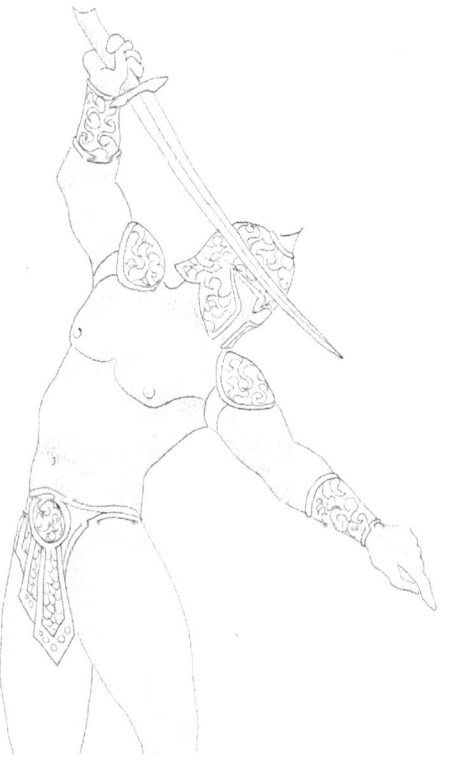

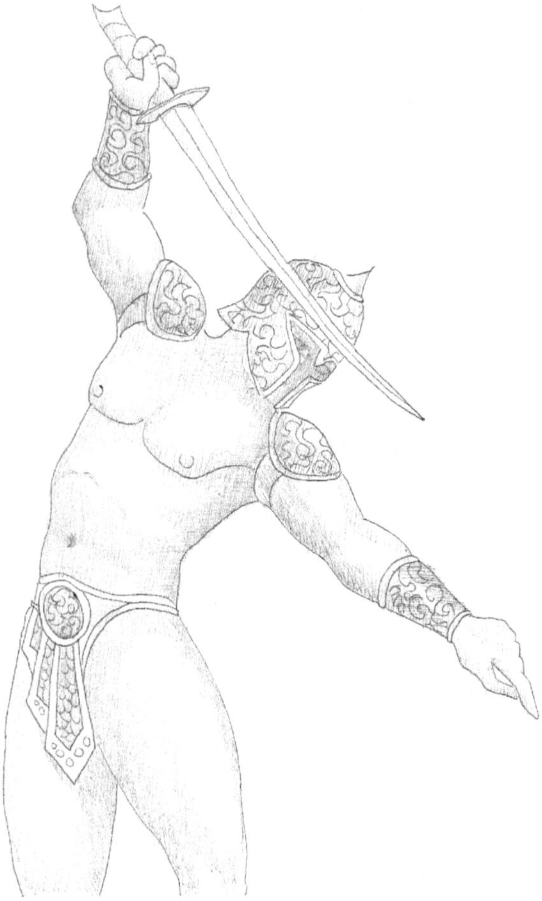

Figure: 3

Slowly intensify the shading.

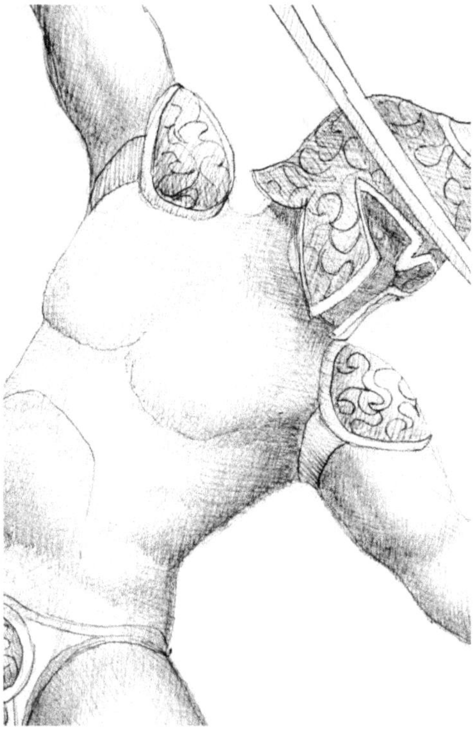

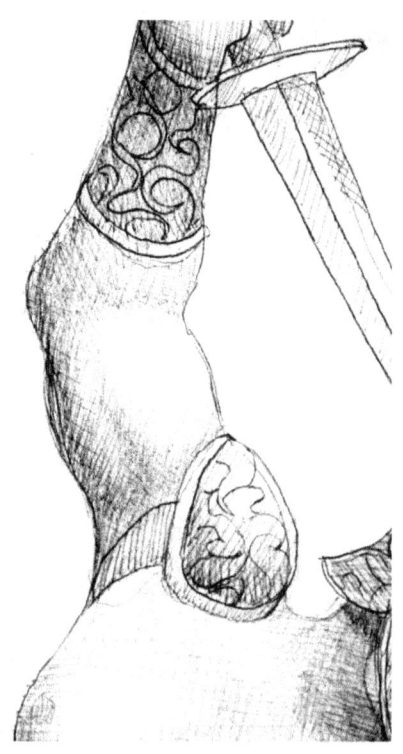

Figures: 4-5

Concentrate the shading on the areas you want to be darker.

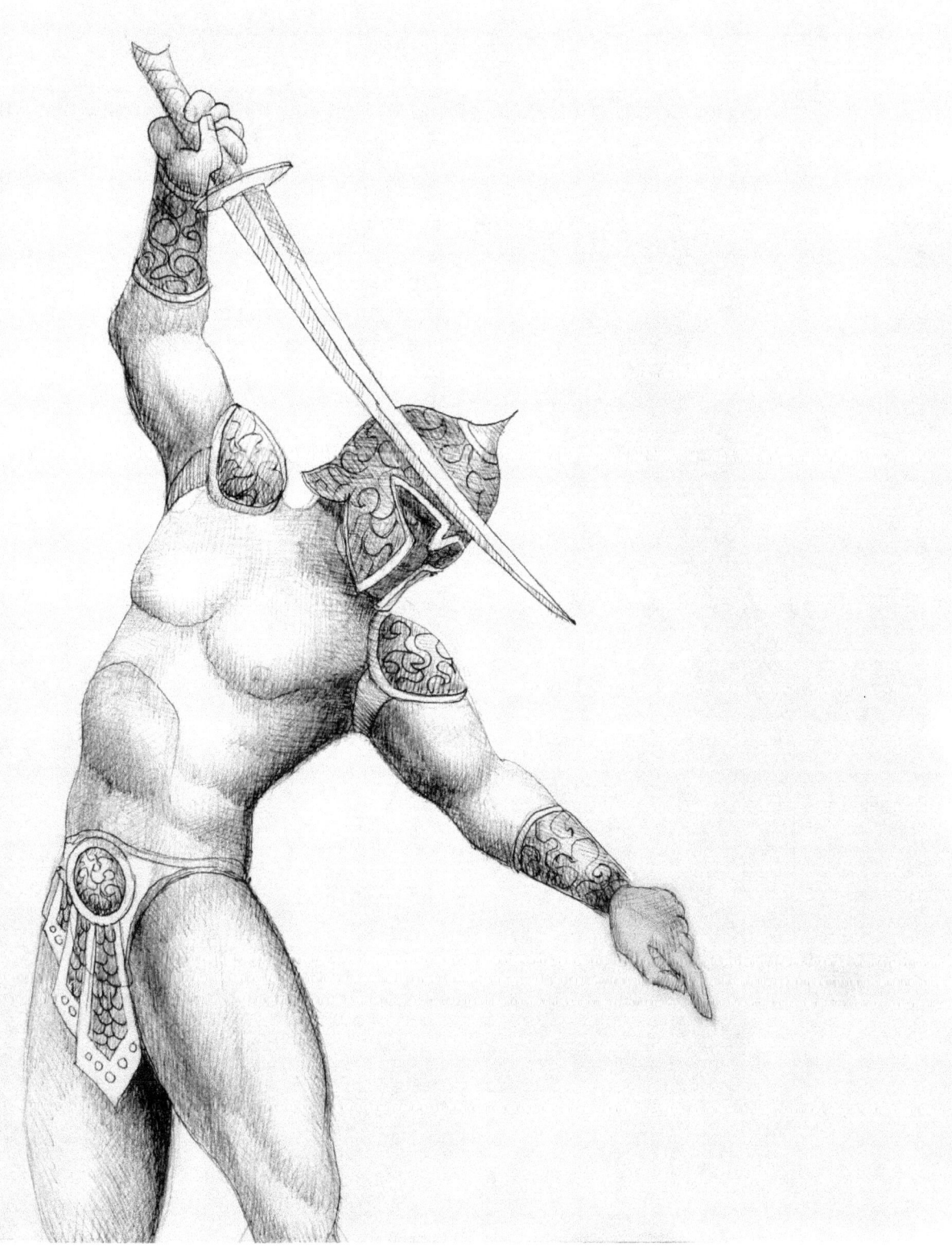

Example Two

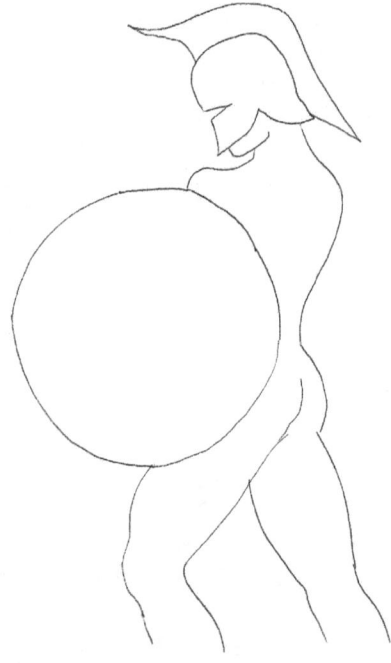

Figure: 1

Once you have a good outline of the figure you can start the shading process.

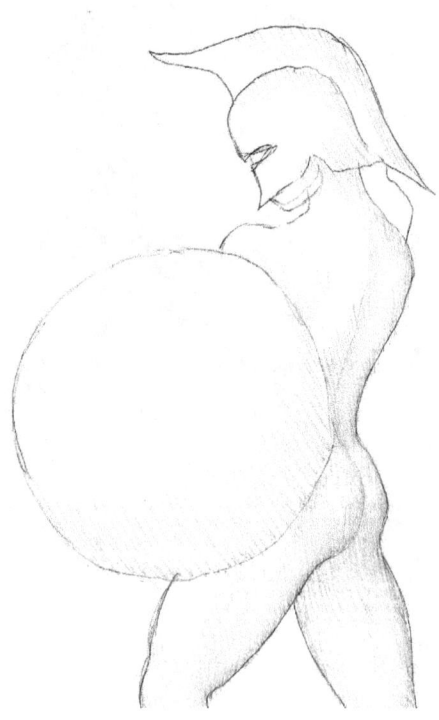

Figure: 2

Start by doing an overall light shading of the entire figure.

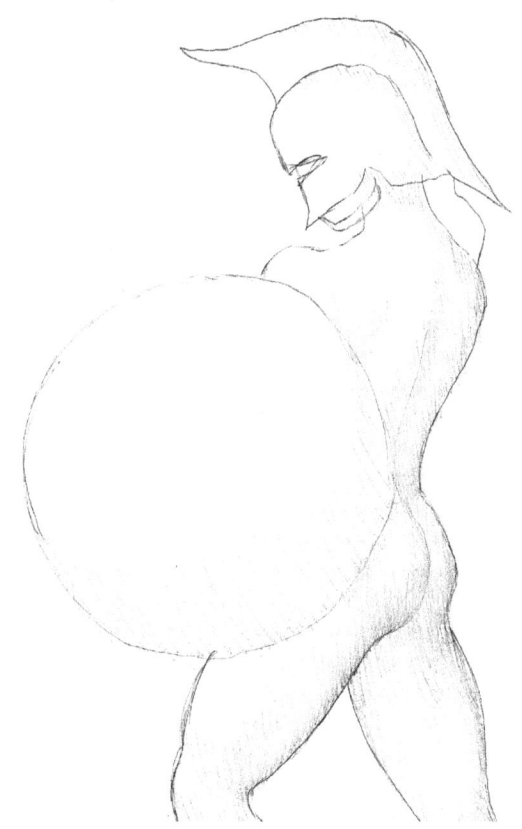

Figure: 3

Gradually intensify the shaded areas.

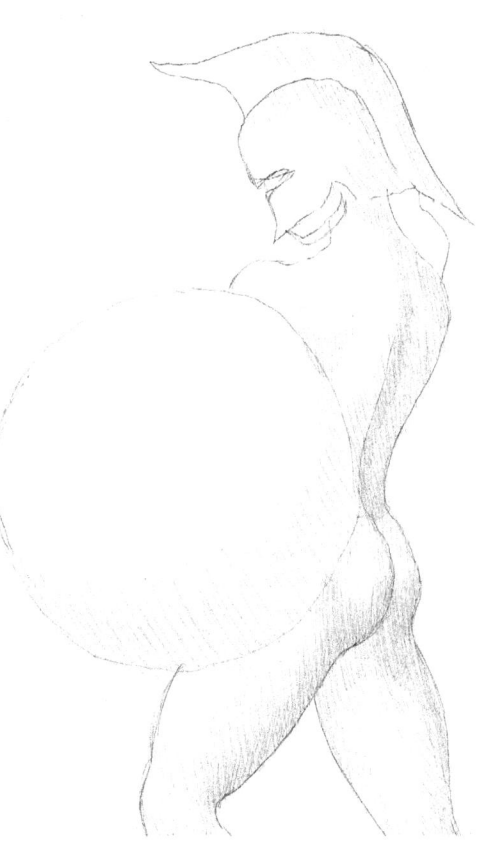

Figure: 4

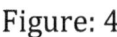 Work slowly and gradually into the shaded parts of the figure.

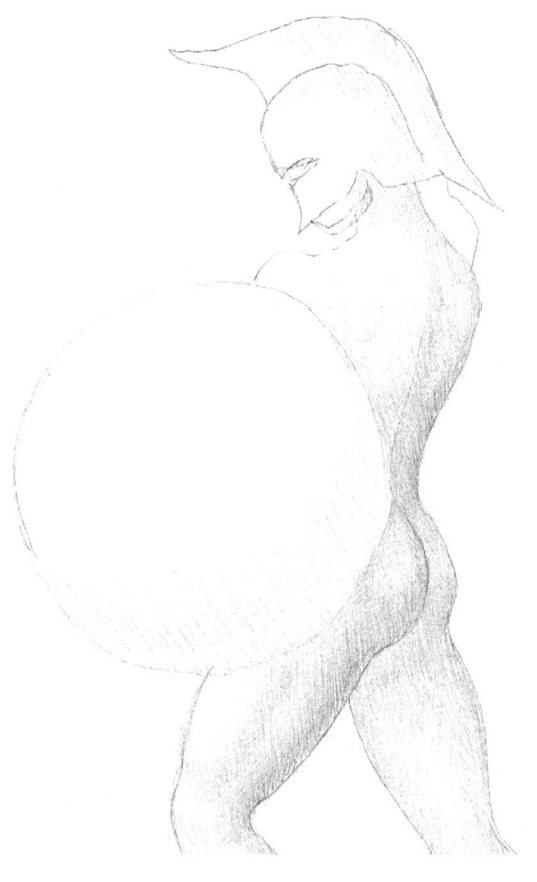

Figure: 5

Concentrate on the darkest areas of the shadow. This will give the figure more depth.

Figure: 6

It is up to you as to how much shadow you want. You can make the figure look more dramatic by exaggerating the dark areas.

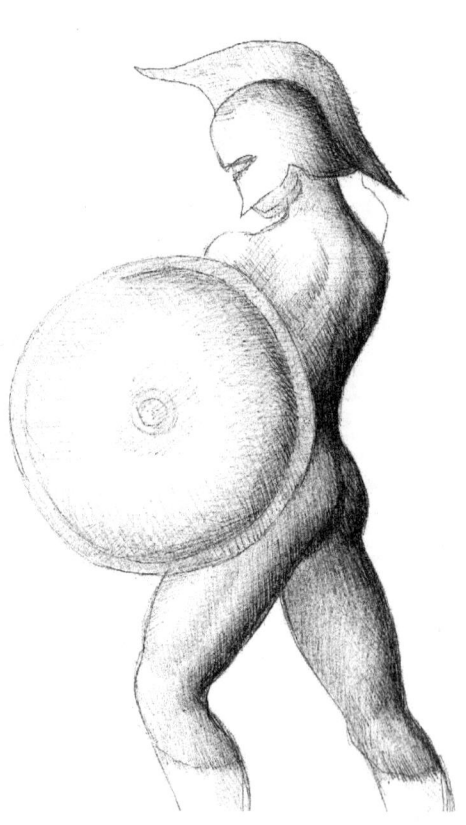

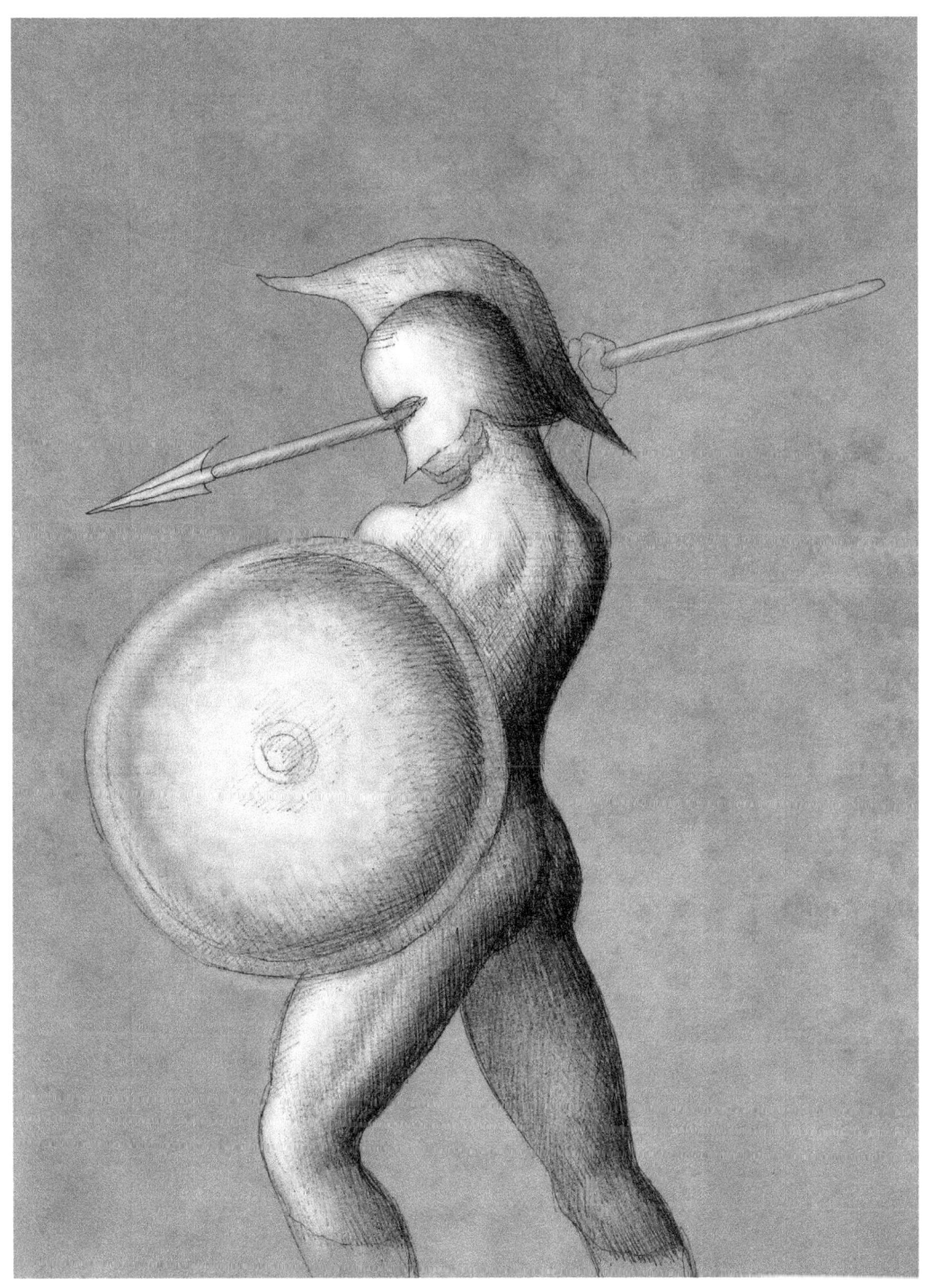

Chapter 6
Drawing Weapons

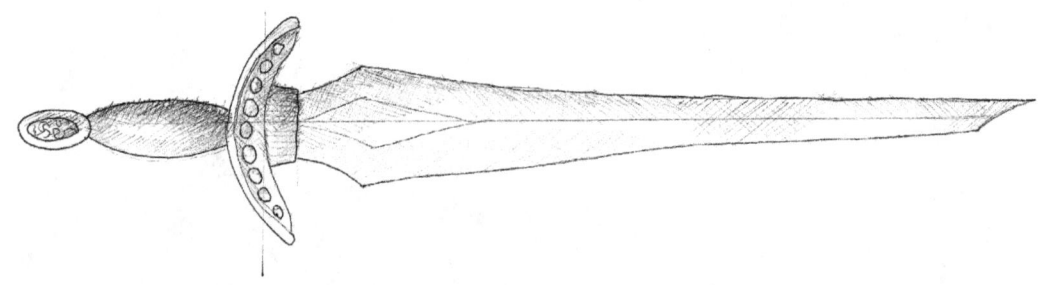

Drawing weapons is very easy it just takes some practice. In fantasy art you can be historically accurate or you can just let your imagination take over, it is totally up to the artist. I like to use a little of both and I do refer back to actual weapons as a guide.

You can be as creative as you like when it comes to drawing weapons. For instance, you can draw them oversized to emphasize the strength of the character. The weapon can be highly decorated and ornate, with skulls or jewels. You can draw them futuristically, or exotic, or scary.

Remember to practice drawing the weapons, then just be creative and have fun. Soon, you will be illustrating your own awesome characters with really cool weapons.

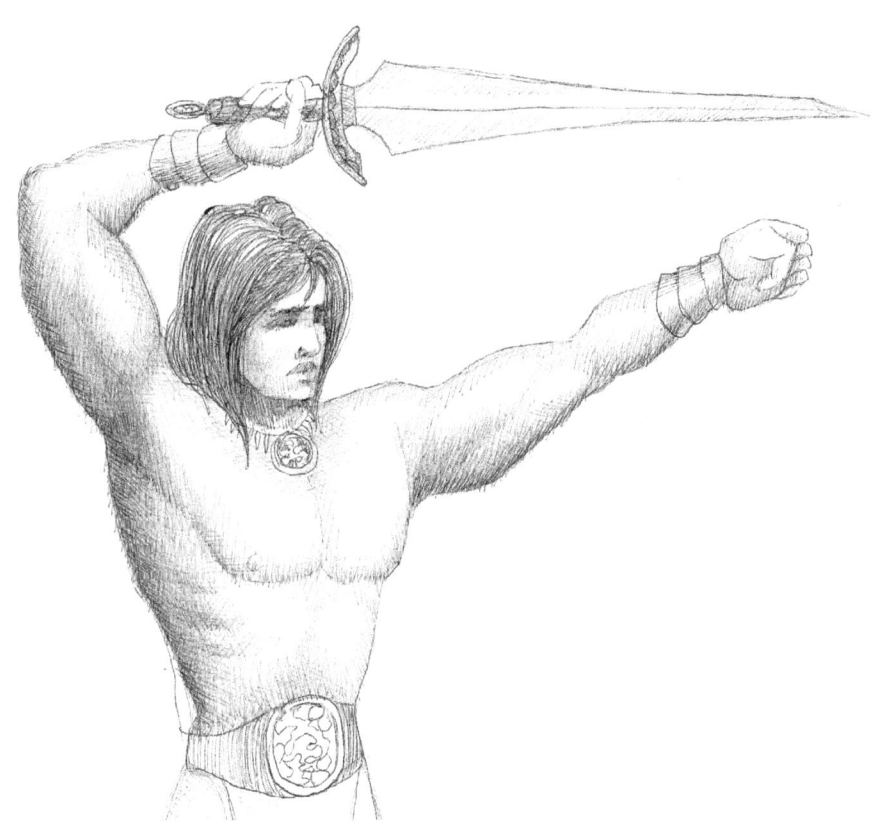

Warrior axe

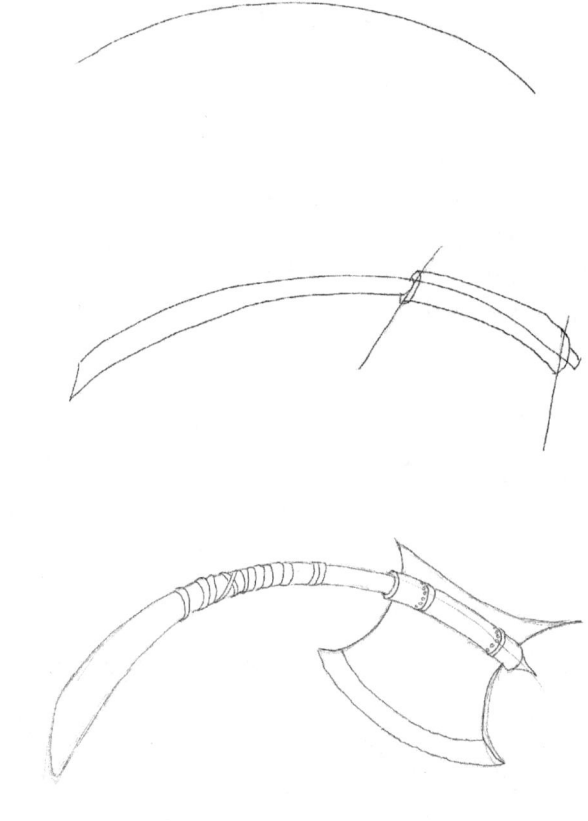

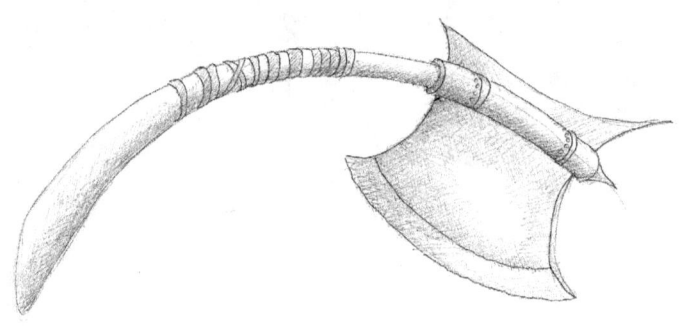

Warrior spear

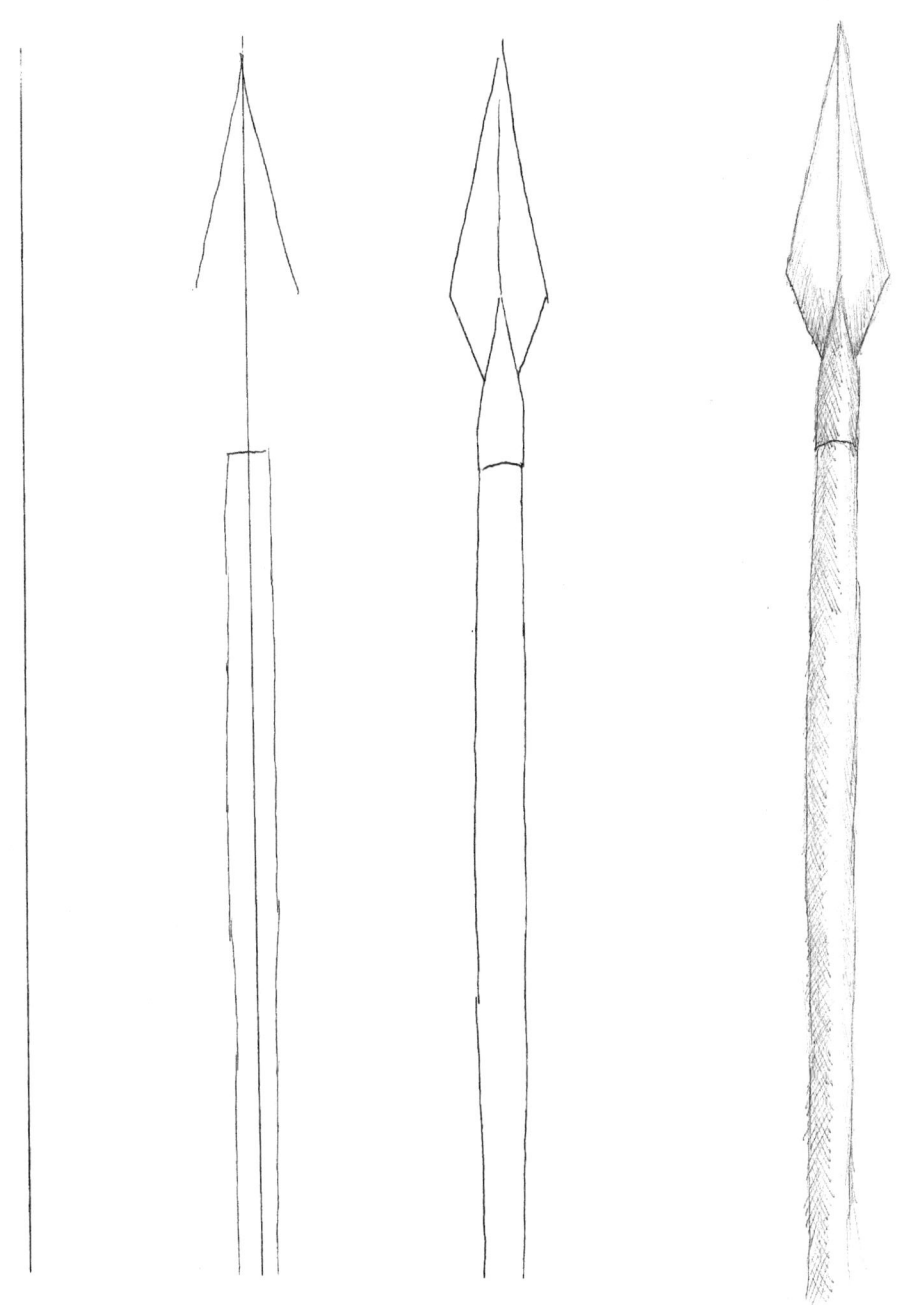

Fancy dagger

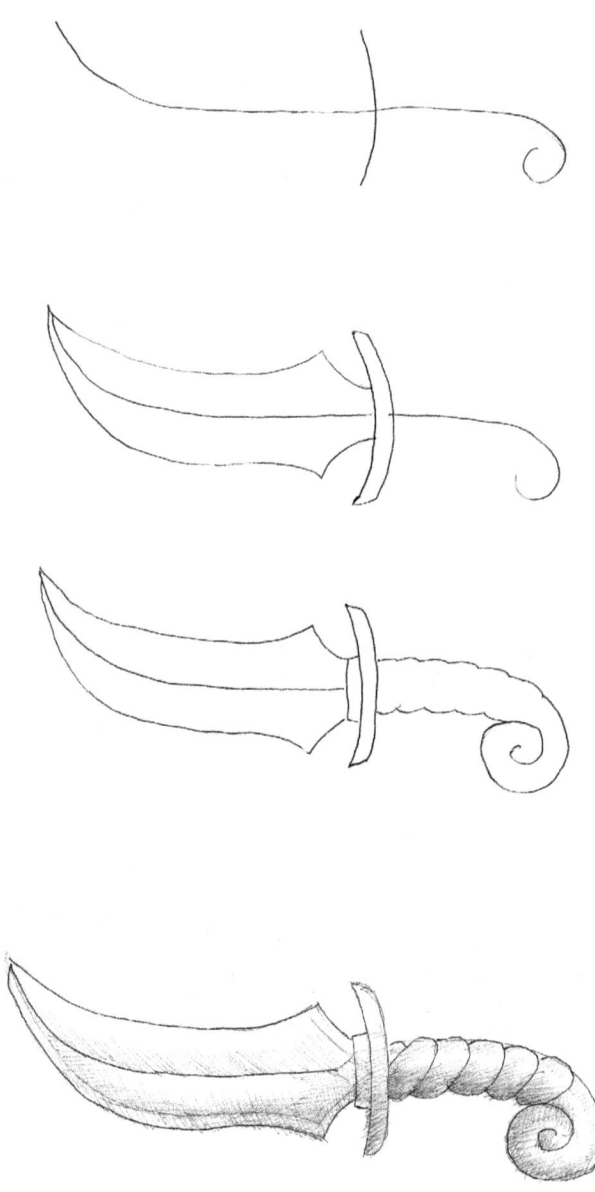

Knife

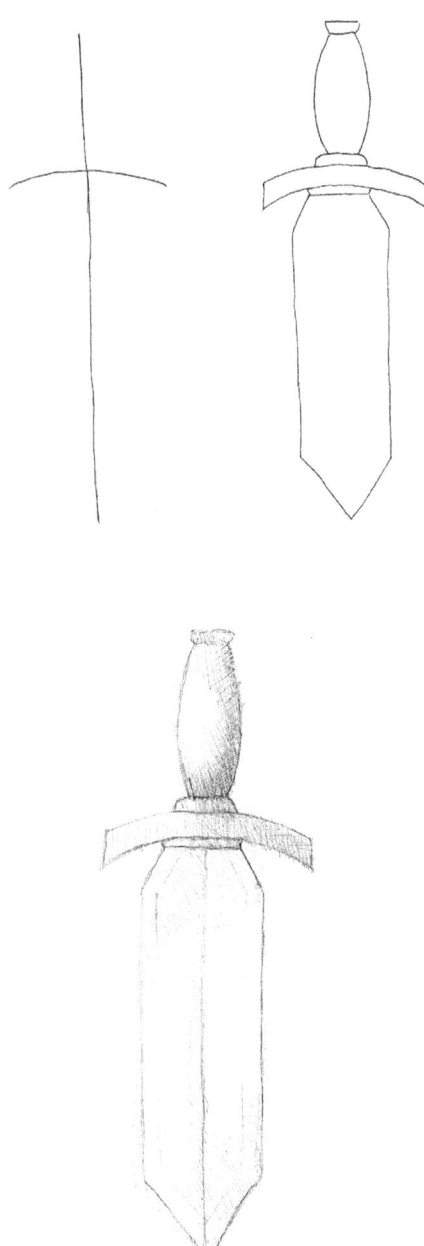

Warrior sword

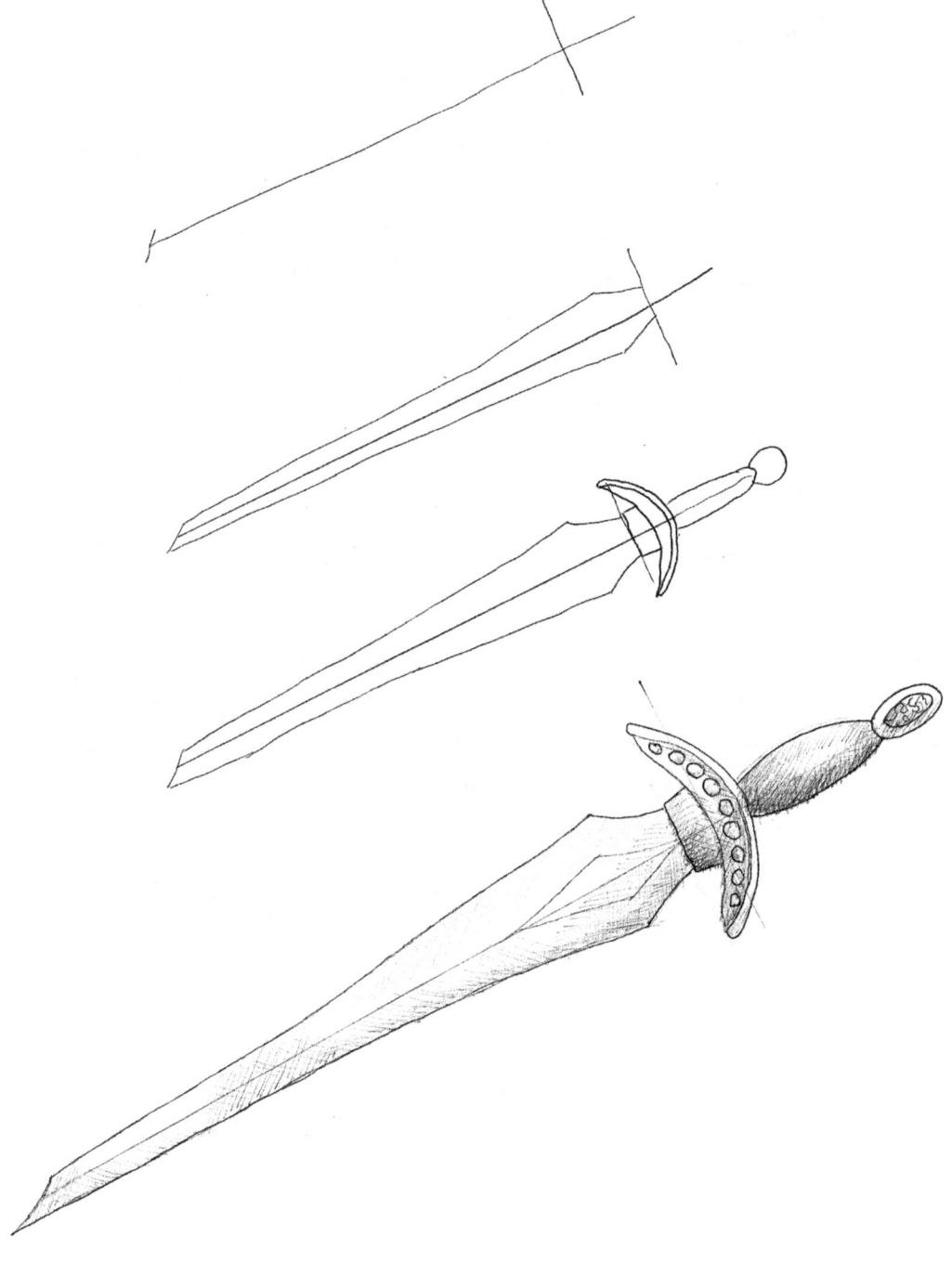

Chapter 7

Drawing examples

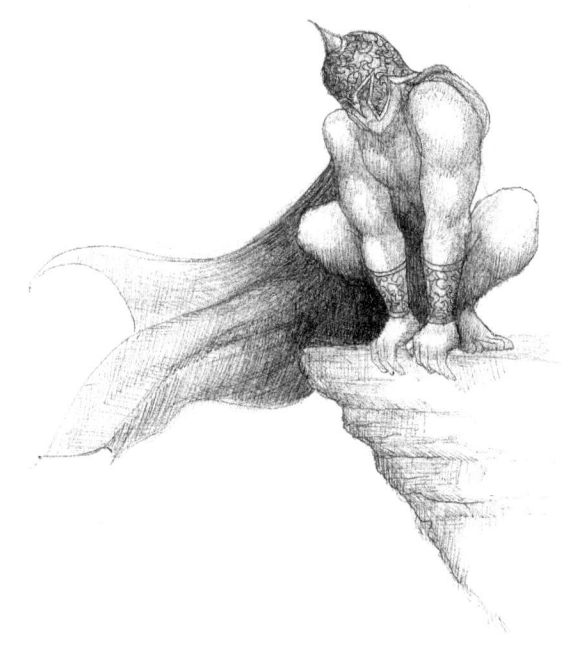

In this section I have included drawings from the beginning stage to the finished drawing to help demonstrate the entire process of drawing. Study the examples and composition of the drawings, I recommend starting the main subject first and then adding in the background. Remember that the best rule to follow is what best works for you.

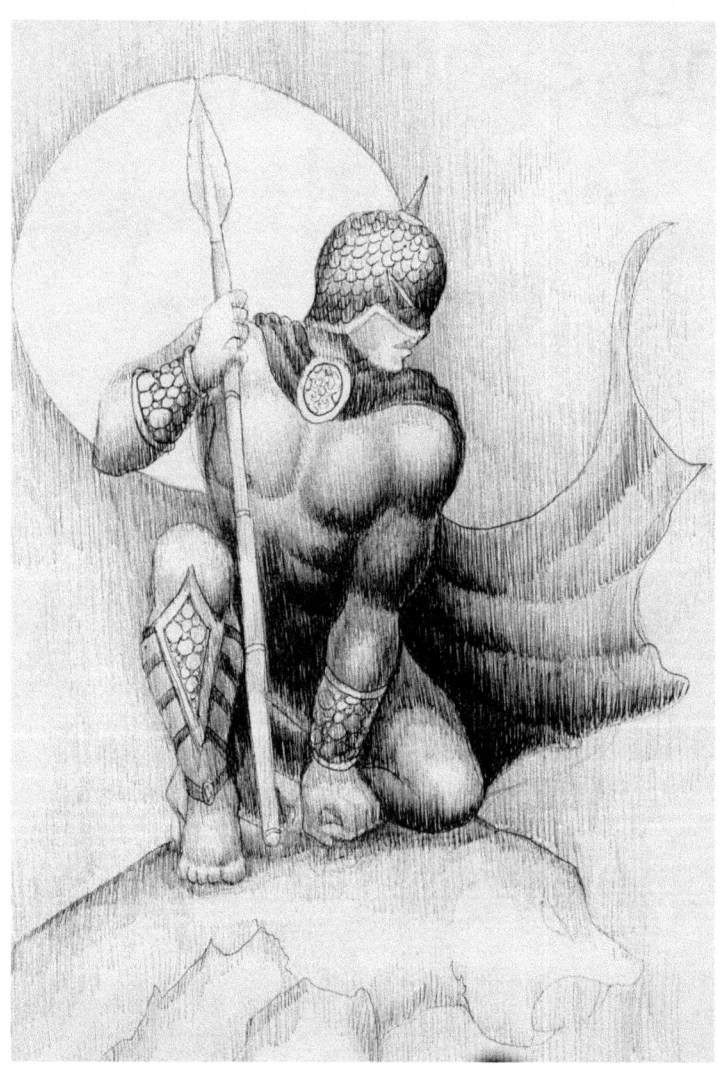

Figure: 1

Select the pose and draw it in using basic circular shapes.

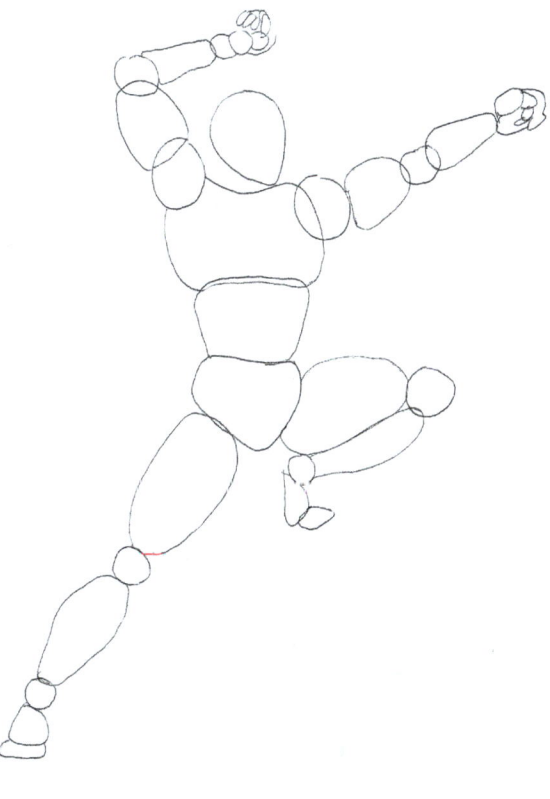

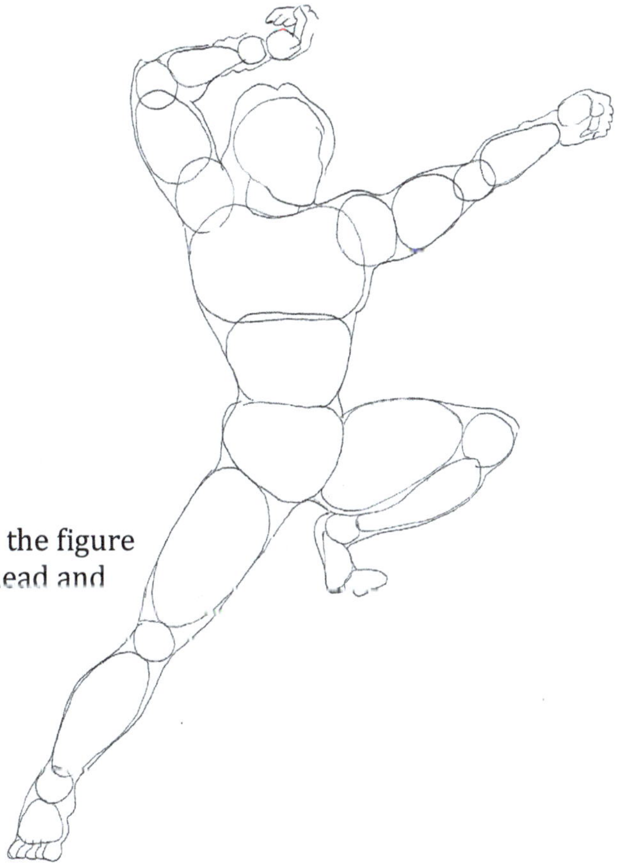

Figure: 2

After you have drawn in the figure using basic shapes, go ahead and outline the entire shape.

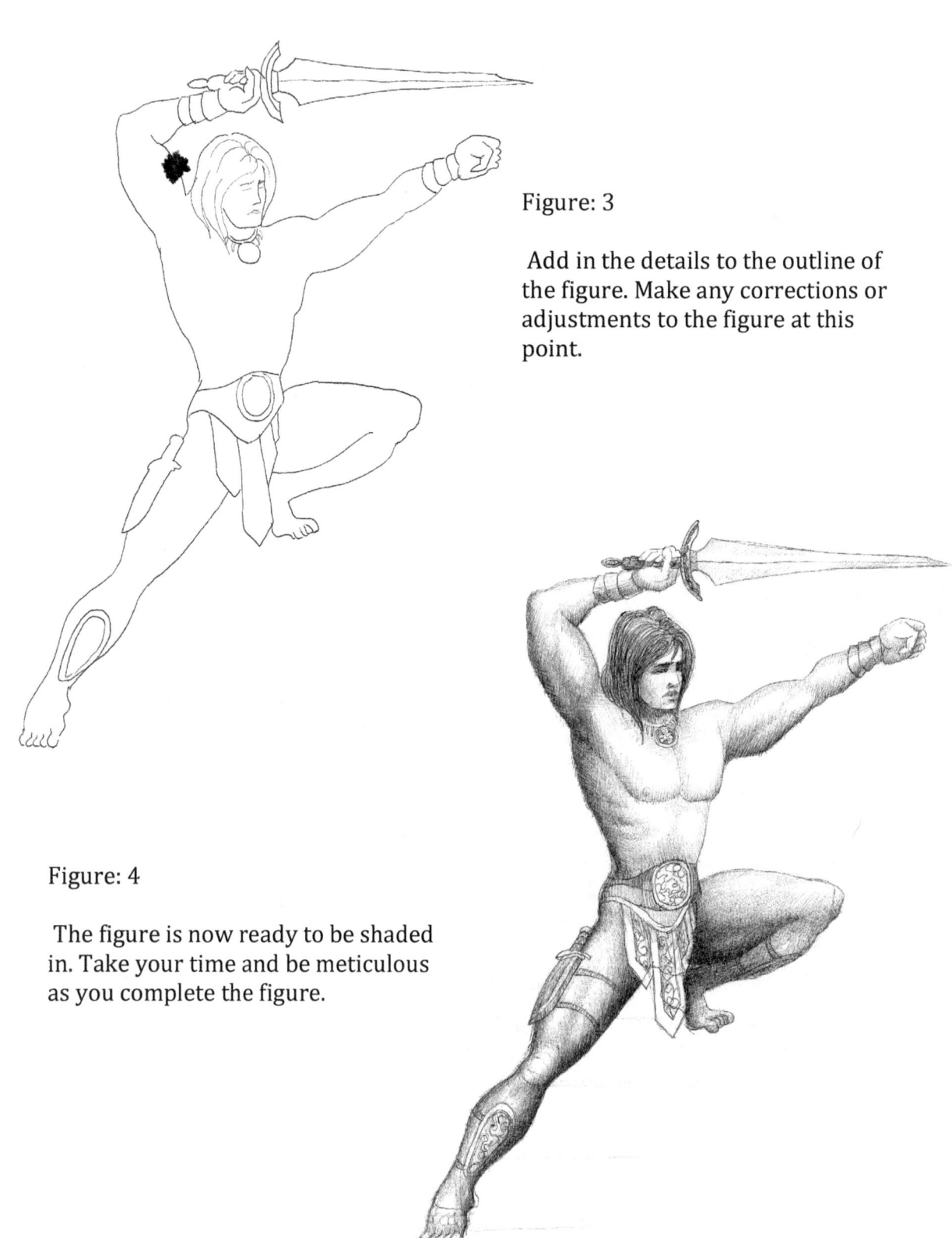

Figure: 3

Add in the details to the outline of the figure. Make any corrections or adjustments to the figure at this point.

Figure: 4

The figure is now ready to be shaded in. Take your time and be meticulous as you complete the figure.

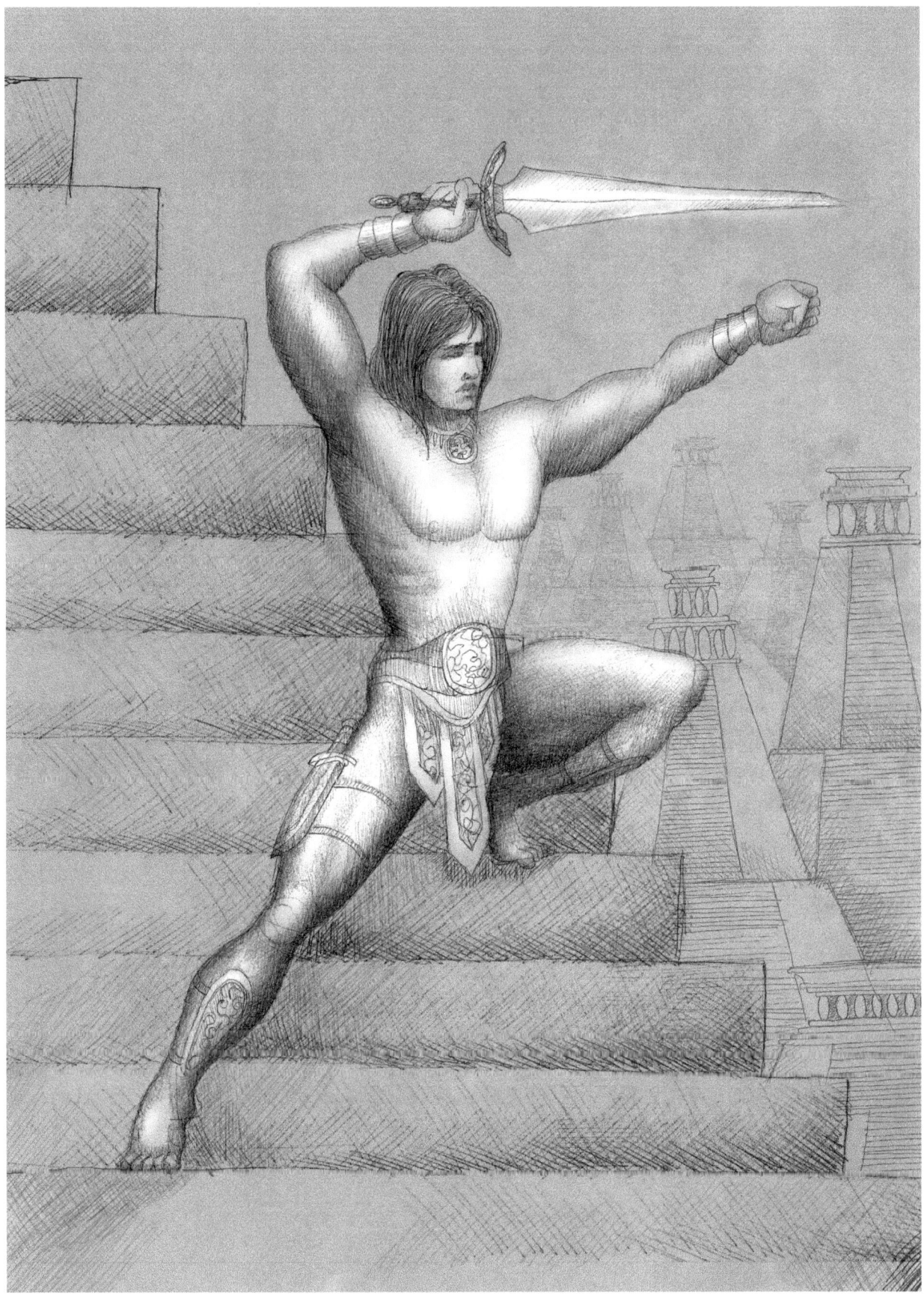

Figure: 1

Draw out the pose by using the basic shapes found in the body. You can refer to the basic shapes of the body chart in chapter 2.

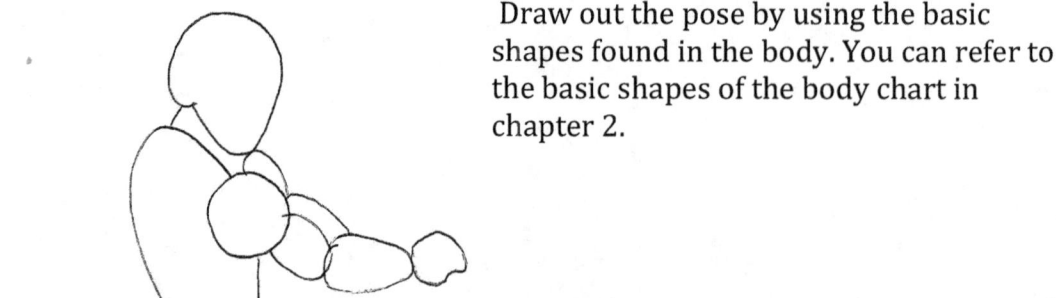

Figure: 2

Pull the shapes together by outlining the entire figure. Keep in mind the shapes of the basic muscle groups as you slowly define the figure.

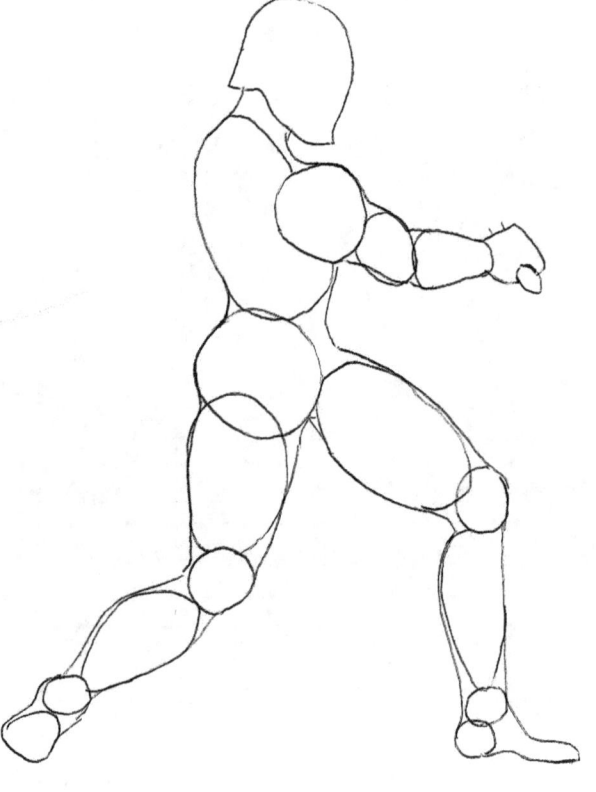

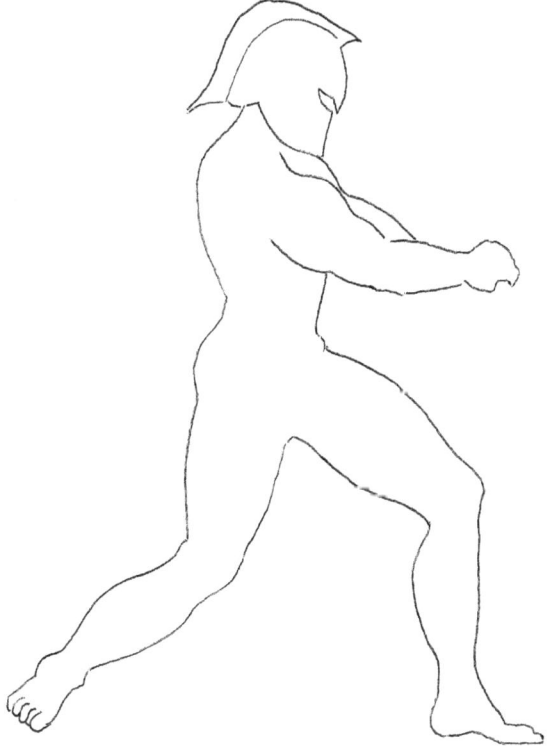

Figure: 3

Make any adjustments or small changes that you want in this stage of the drawing. Make sure the figure looks correct and is the way you want it to look.

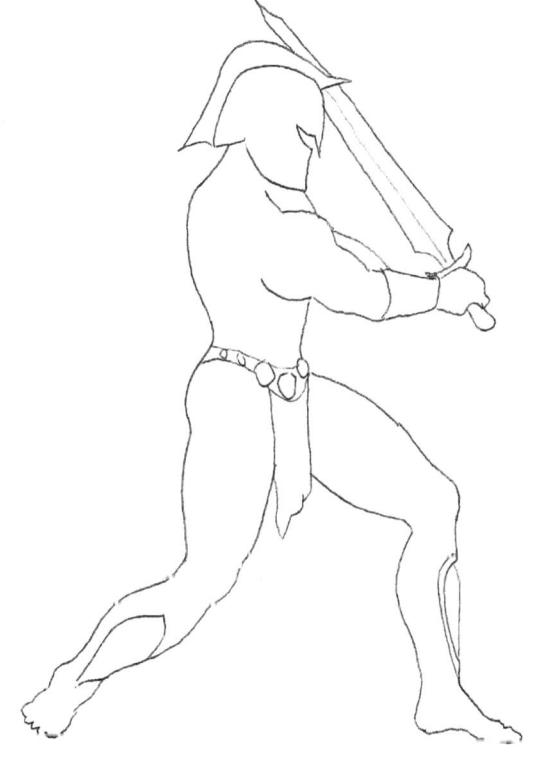

Figure: 4

Add in all the small details that you want to include in your drawing. This will include the costume and armor.

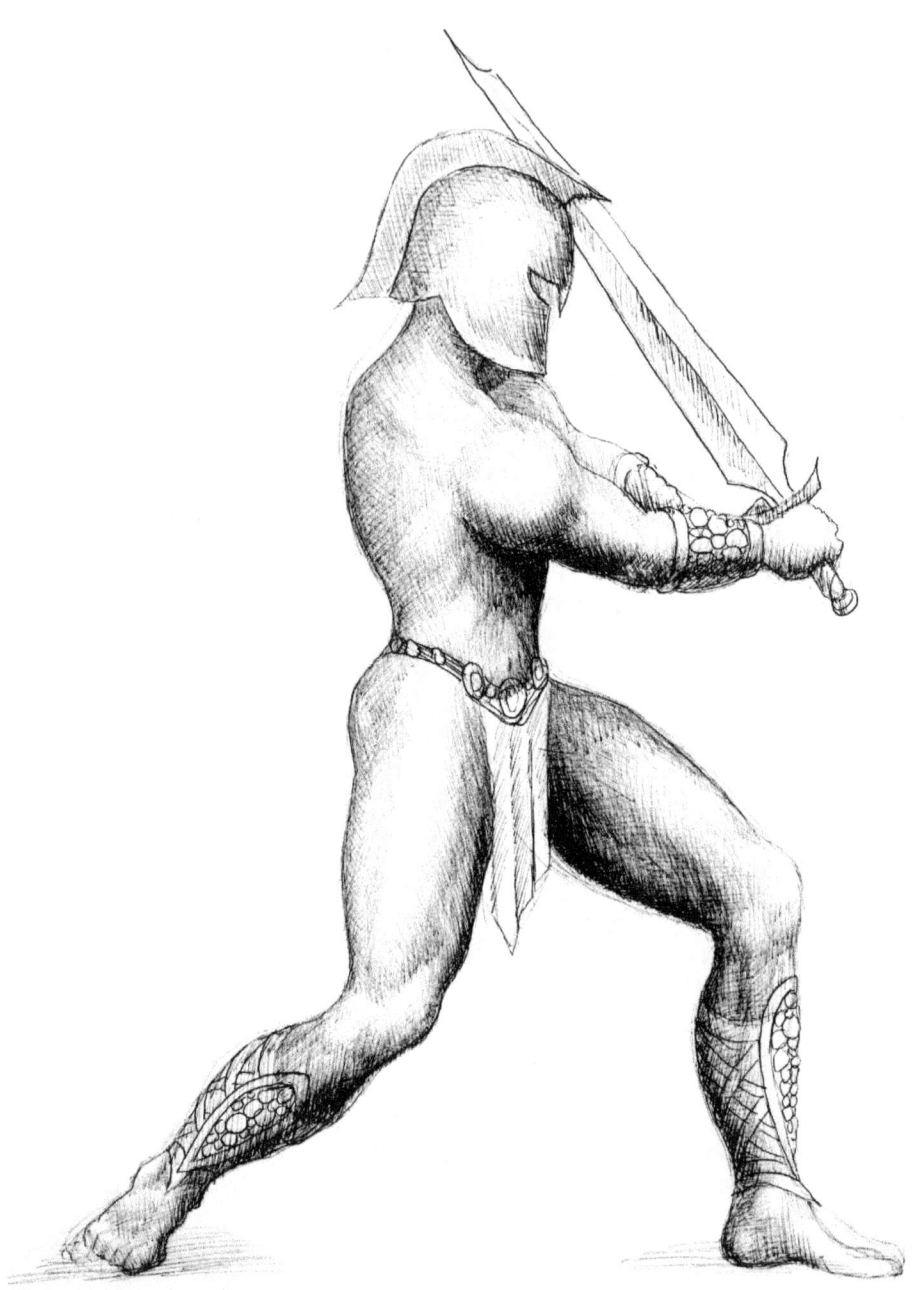

Figure: 5

Start the shading process as lightly as you can in
the beginning. When you have the overall figure
shaded go back and darken and emphasize the
deeper shaded areas.

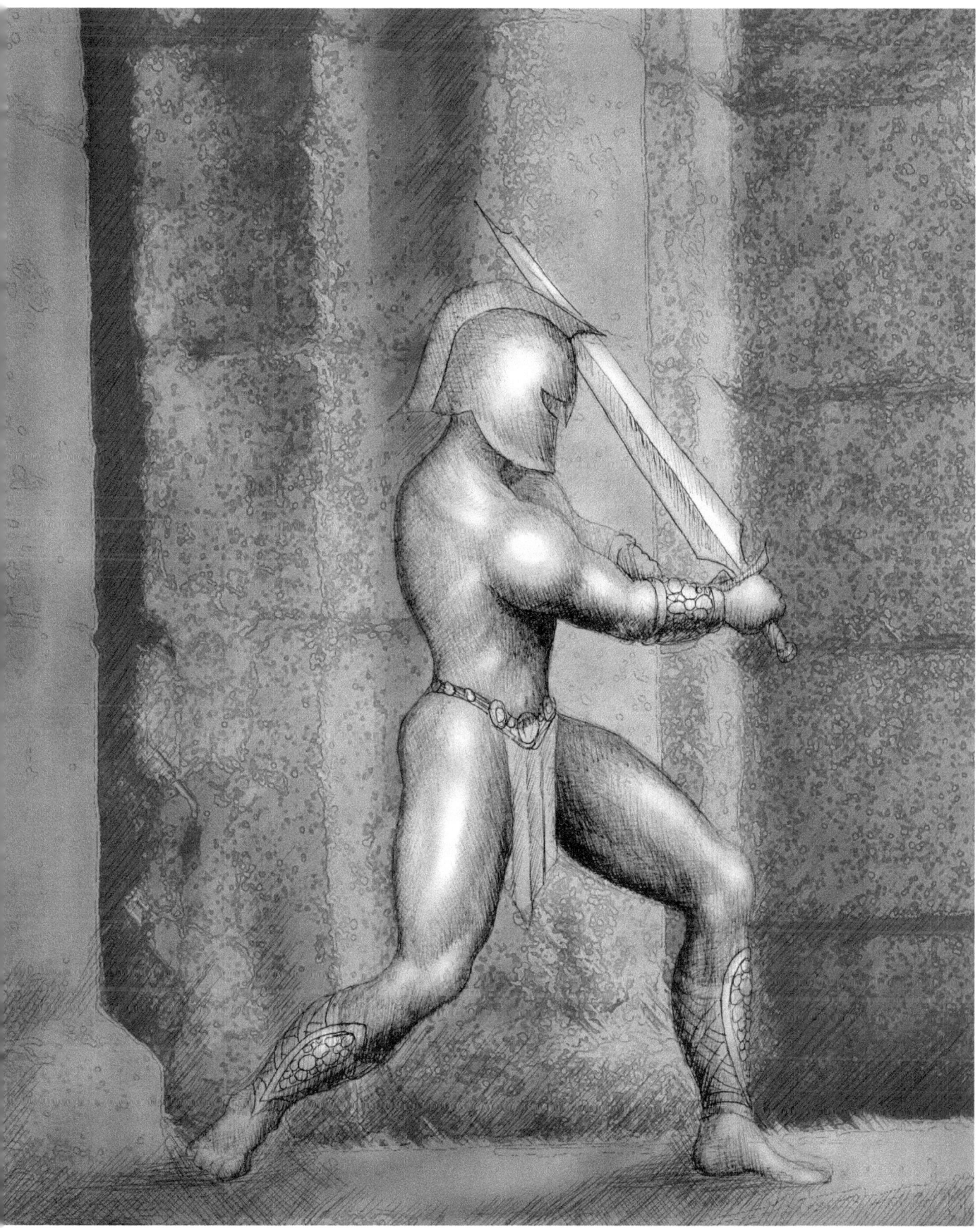

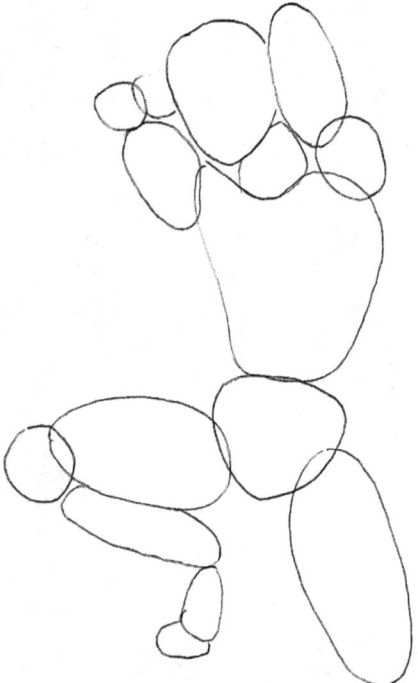

Figure: 1

Once you establish the pose you want to use, draw it out using basic shapes. Use the basic shapes of the body chart to guide you.

Figure: 2

Slowly outline the entire figure. Outline the shapes of the muscles. You can use the basic muscle chart in chapter 2 as a guide.

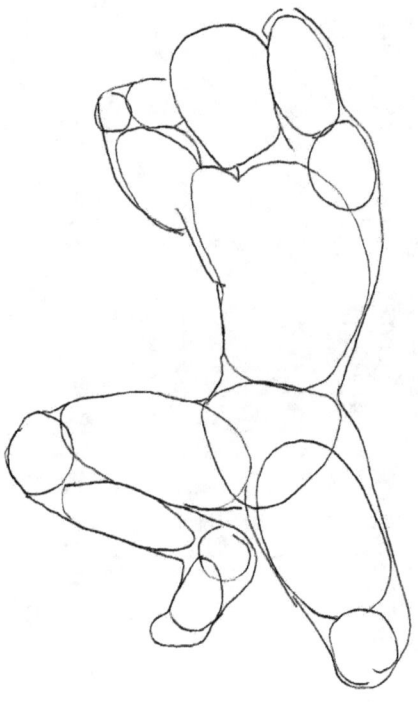

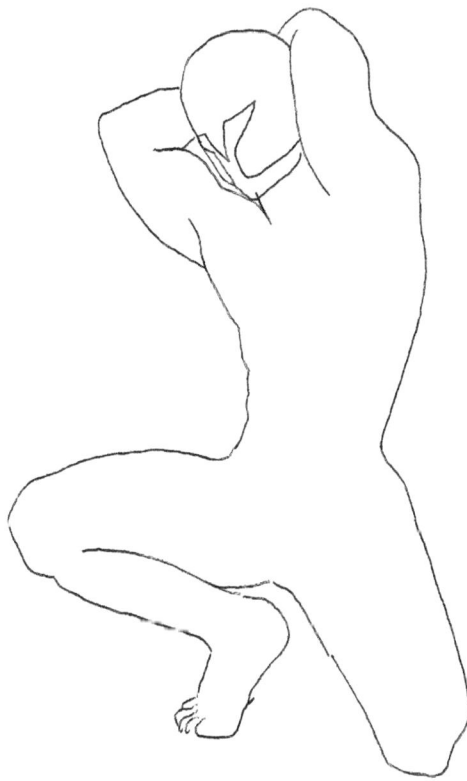

Figure: 3

Once you have a good outline of the figure you can make slight changes before adding the details. For example you might want to make the arm muscles slightly more muscular.

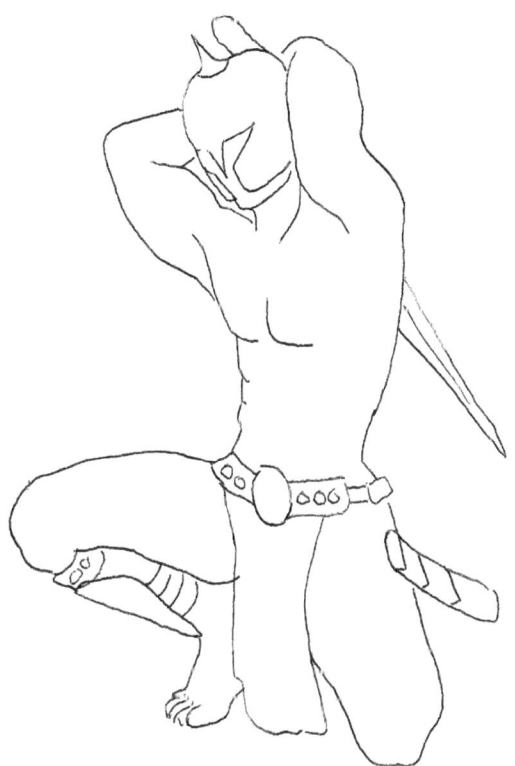

Figure: 4

Now, you can draw in all the small details such as the weapon. You can draw in knee guards or chest armor.

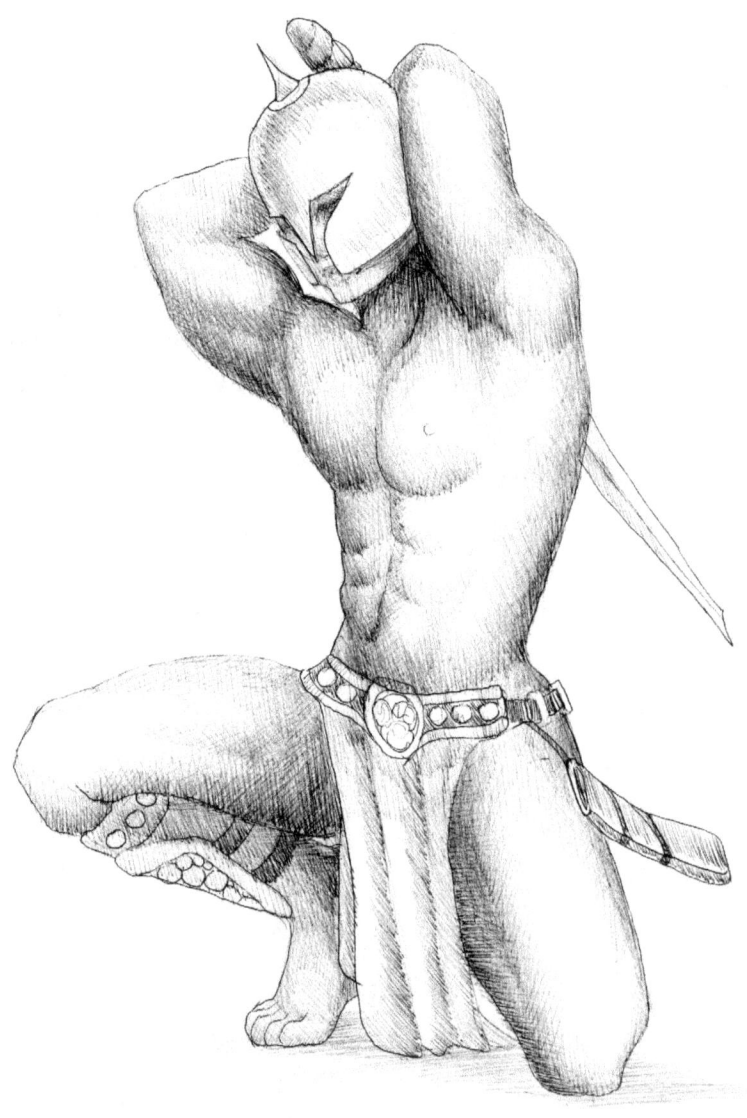

Figure: 5

Establish your light source and direction and
begin shading. Shade in the actual muscle
groups that compose the body. Shade the
entire figure then go back and shade in the
areas you want to be the darkest.

Finally, finish the drawing by adding a
background and foreground.

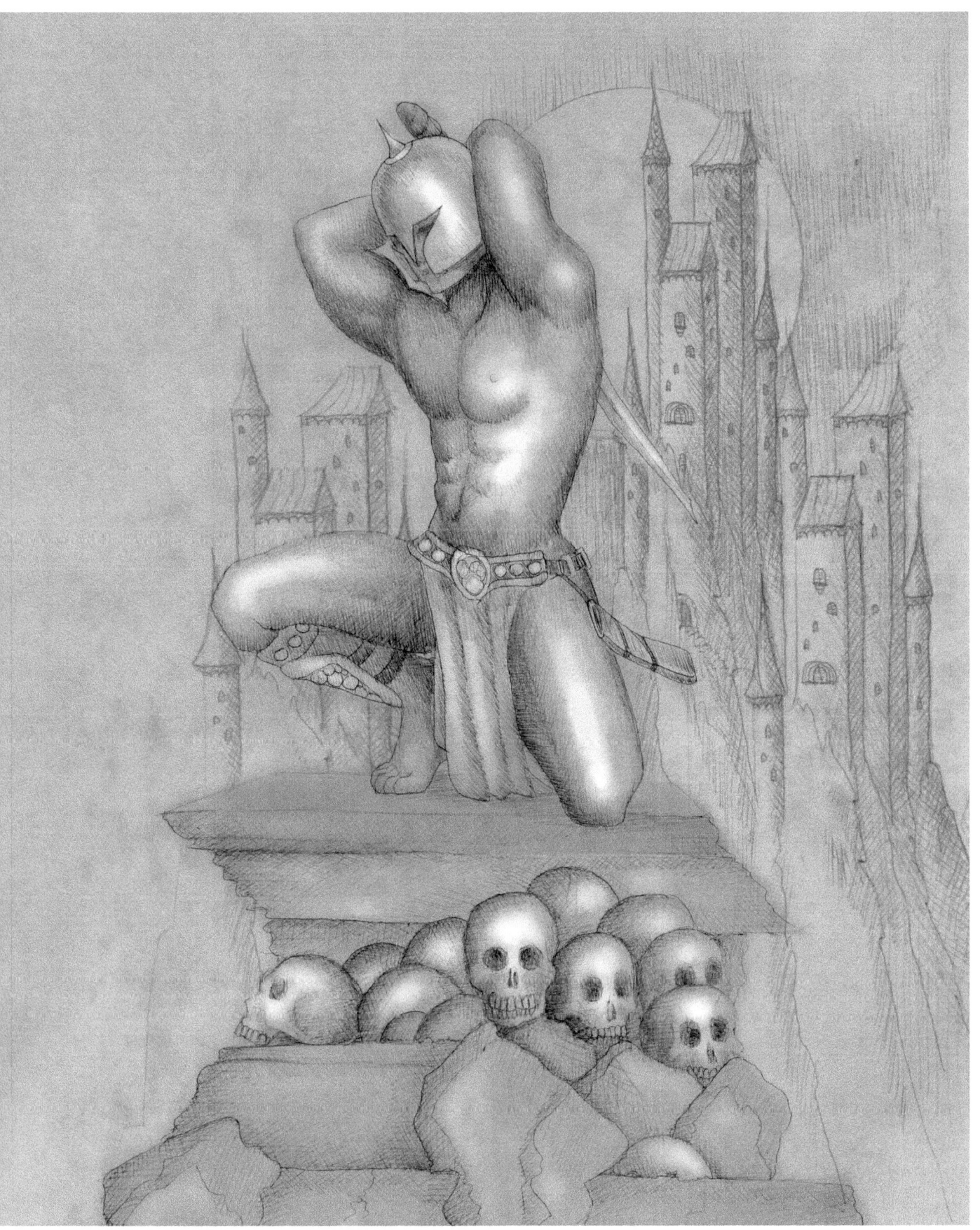

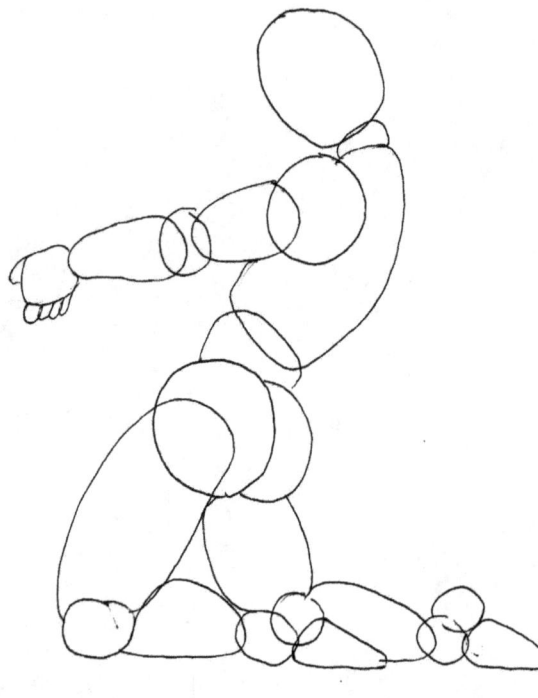

Figure: 1

Render the pose in basic shapes. This allows you to make small adjustments to the overall shape of the drawing.

Figure: 2

Outline the entire shape. Make sure to keep the lines fluid and flowing as you make your outline.

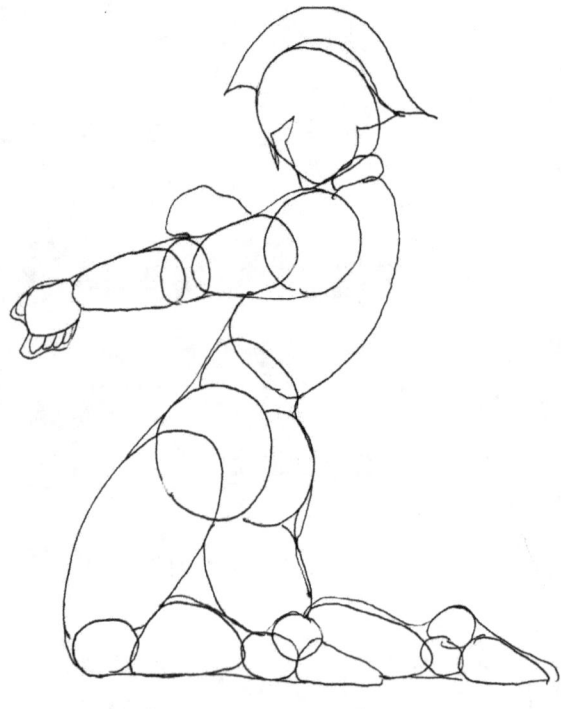

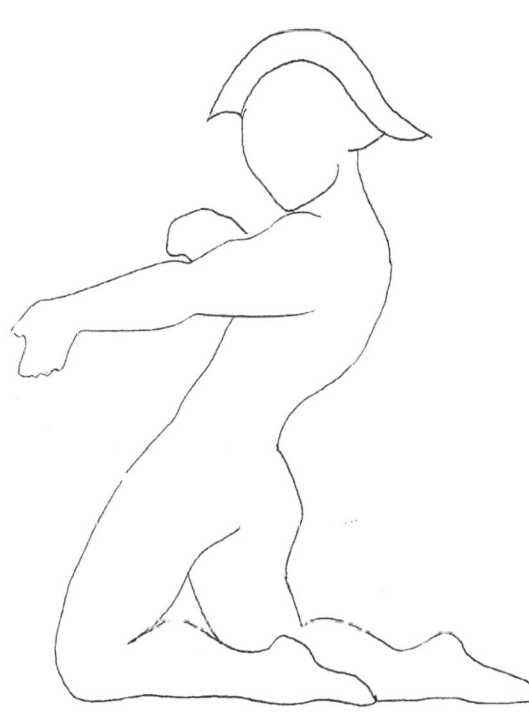

Figure: 3

Tighten up and clean the lines, then pull everything together.

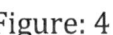

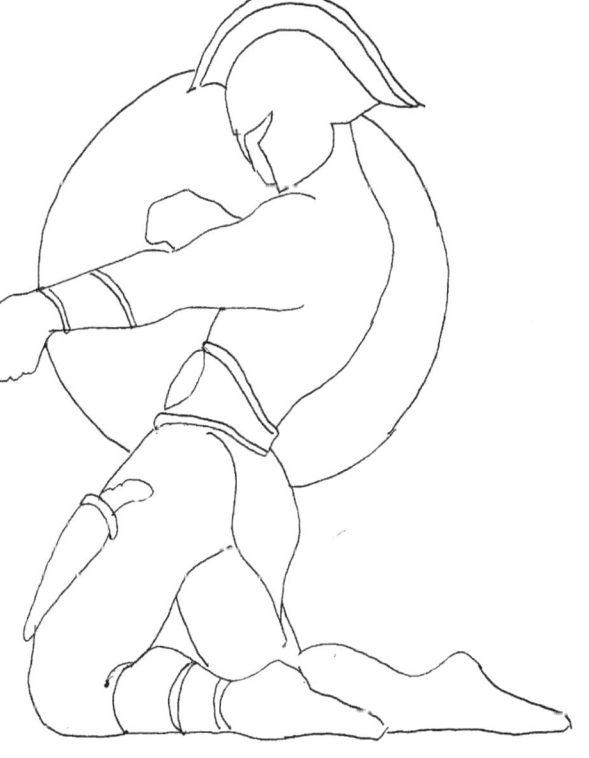

Figure: 4

Draw in all the intricate and delicate detail.

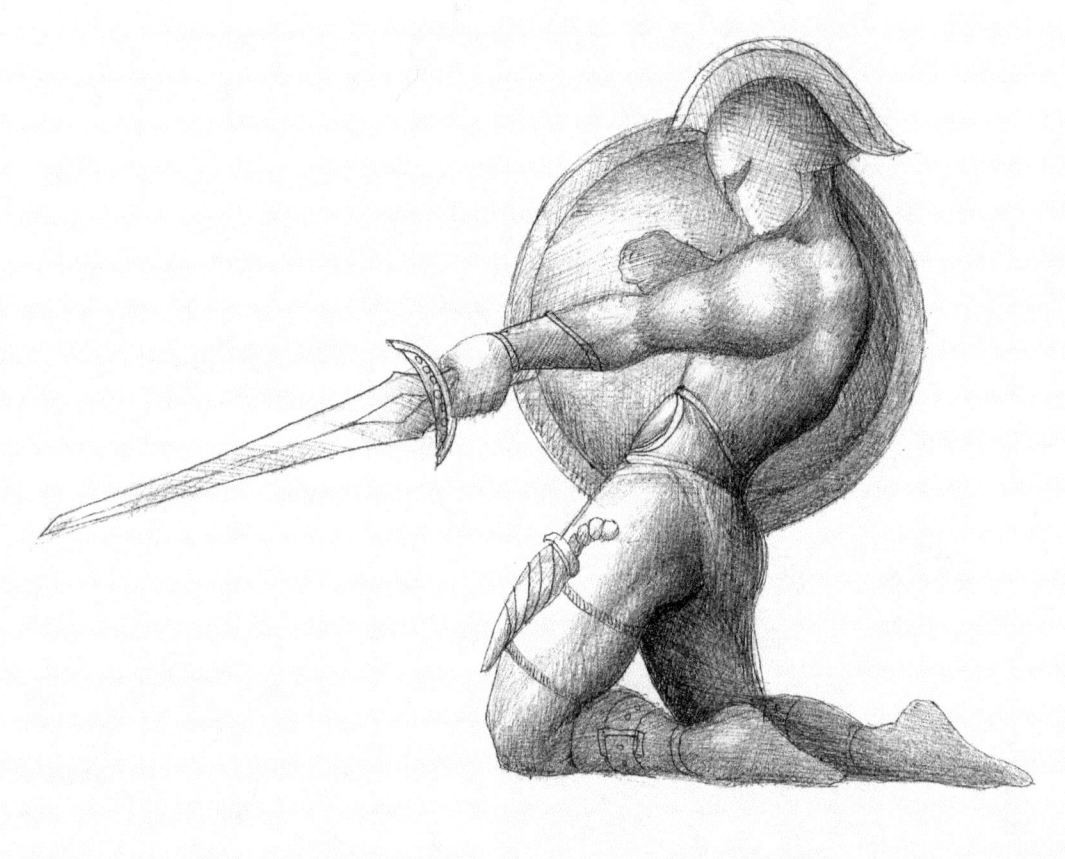

Figure: 5

Once you have established your light direction you can start the shading process.

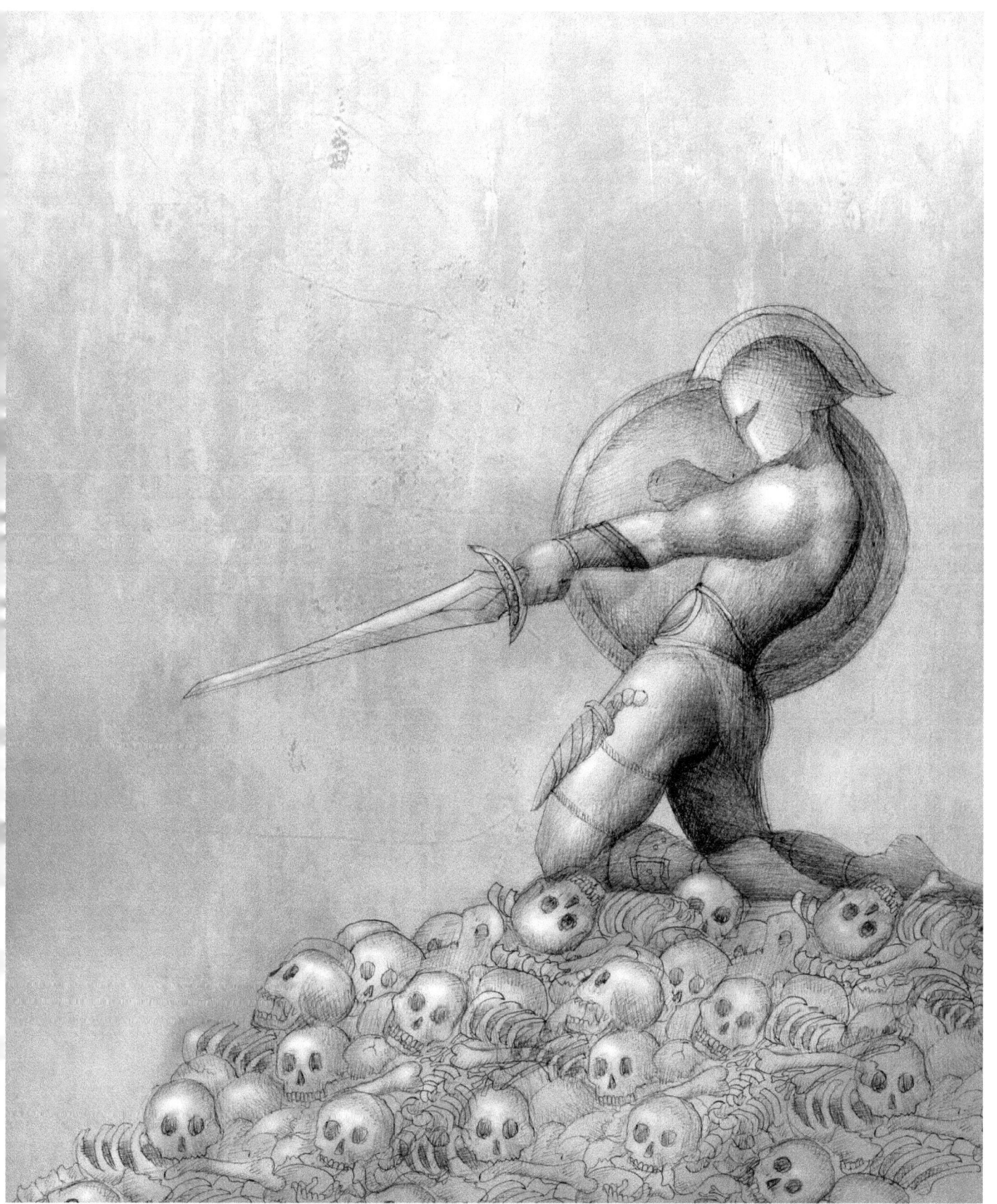

Figure: 1

Draw the pose by using small shapes.

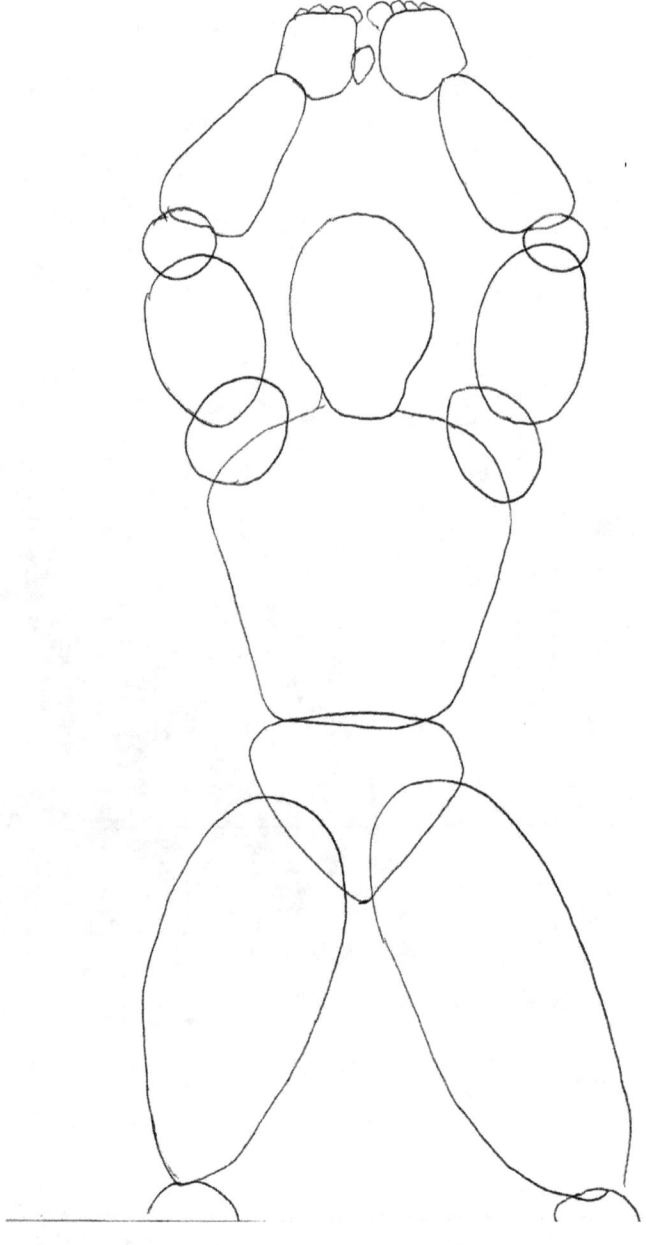

Figure: 2

Outline the shapes to from the entire figure.

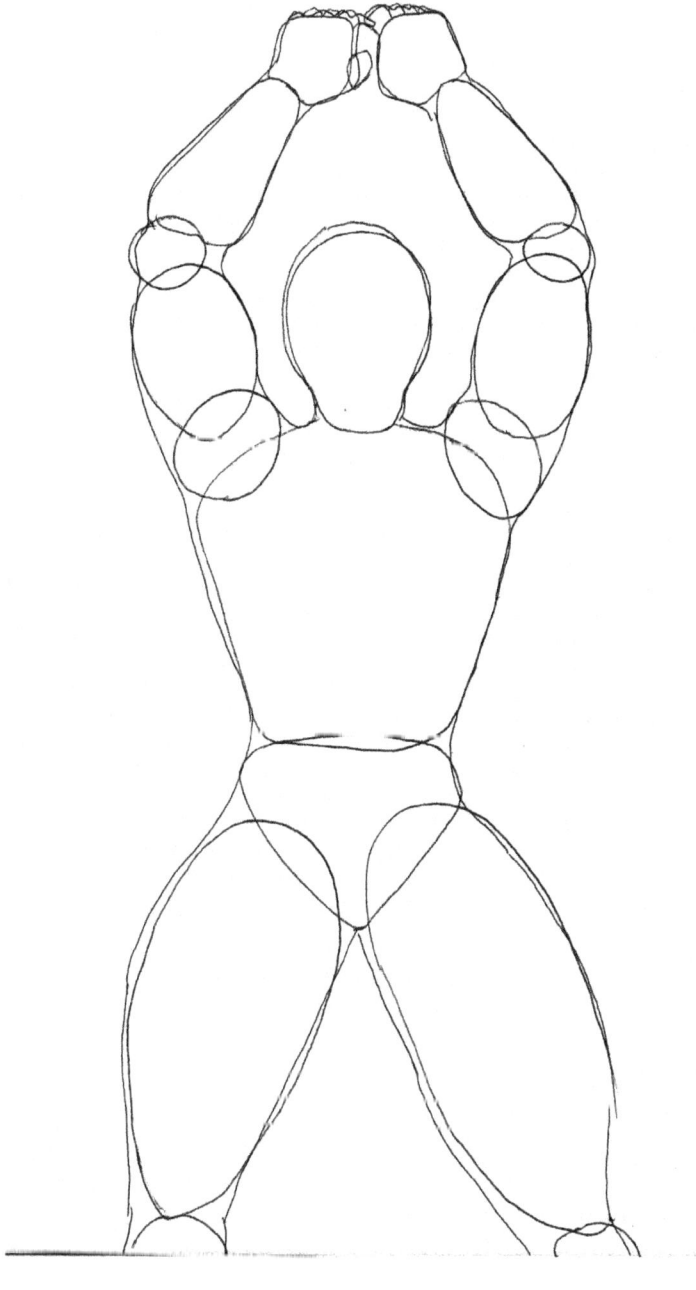

Figure: 3

Make any small adjustments and
corrections at this stage.

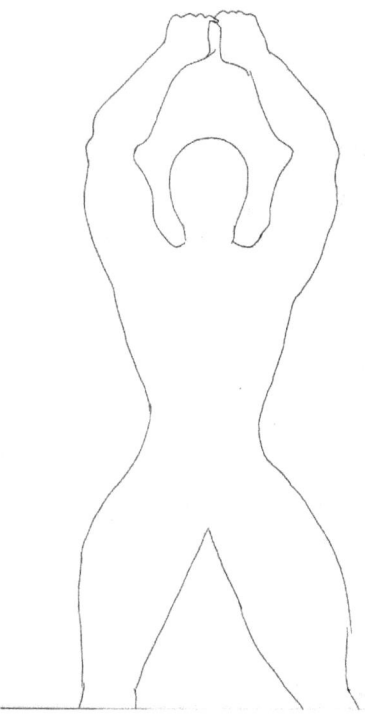

Figure: 4

Draw all the costume details and
all the prop details.

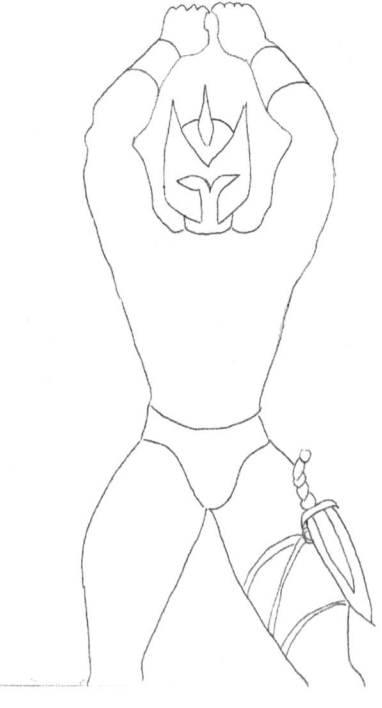

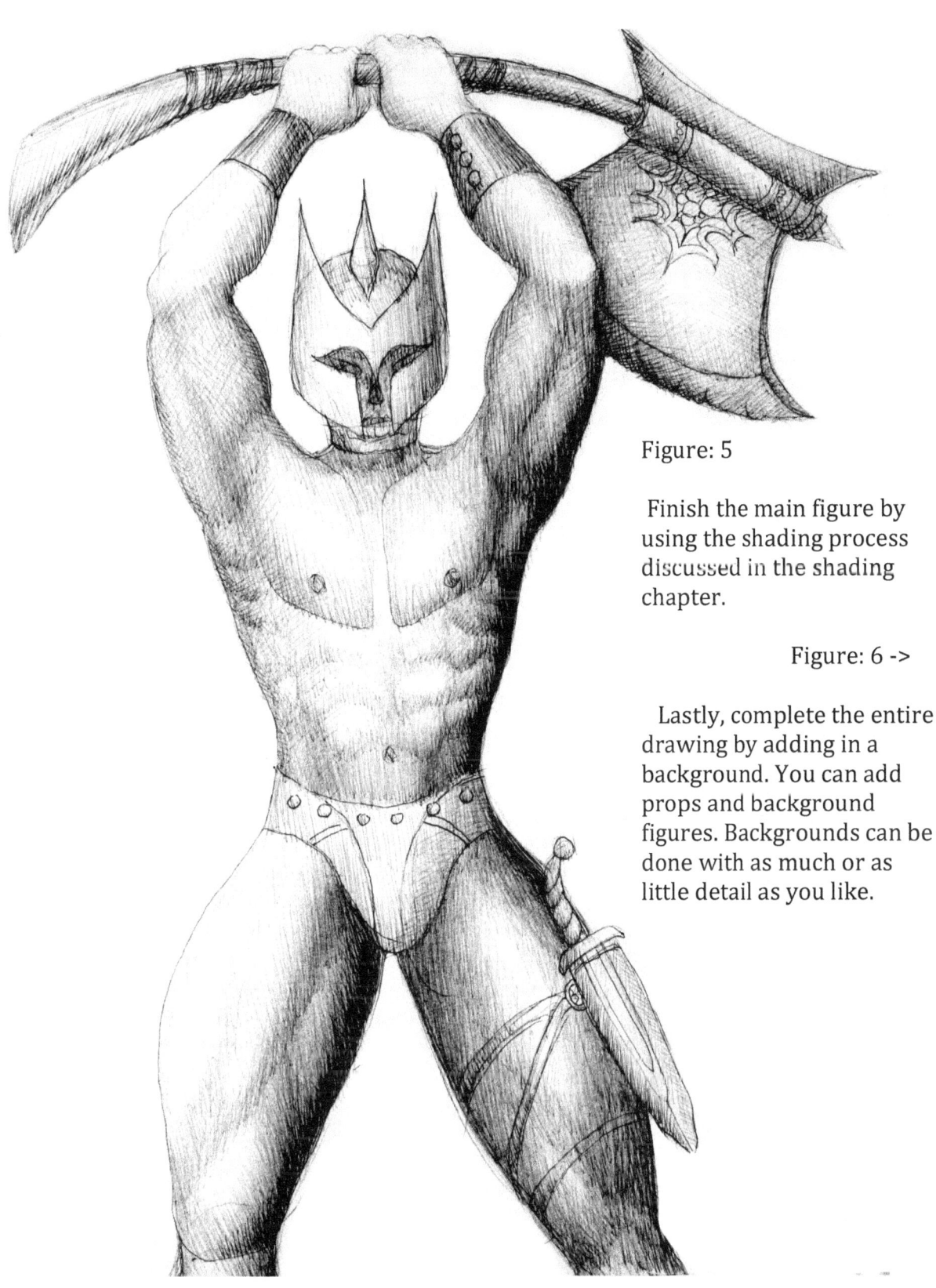

Figure: 5

Finish the main figure by using the shading process discussed in the shading chapter.

Figure: 6 ->

Lastly, complete the entire drawing by adding in a background. You can add props and background figures. Backgrounds can be done with as much or as little detail as you like.

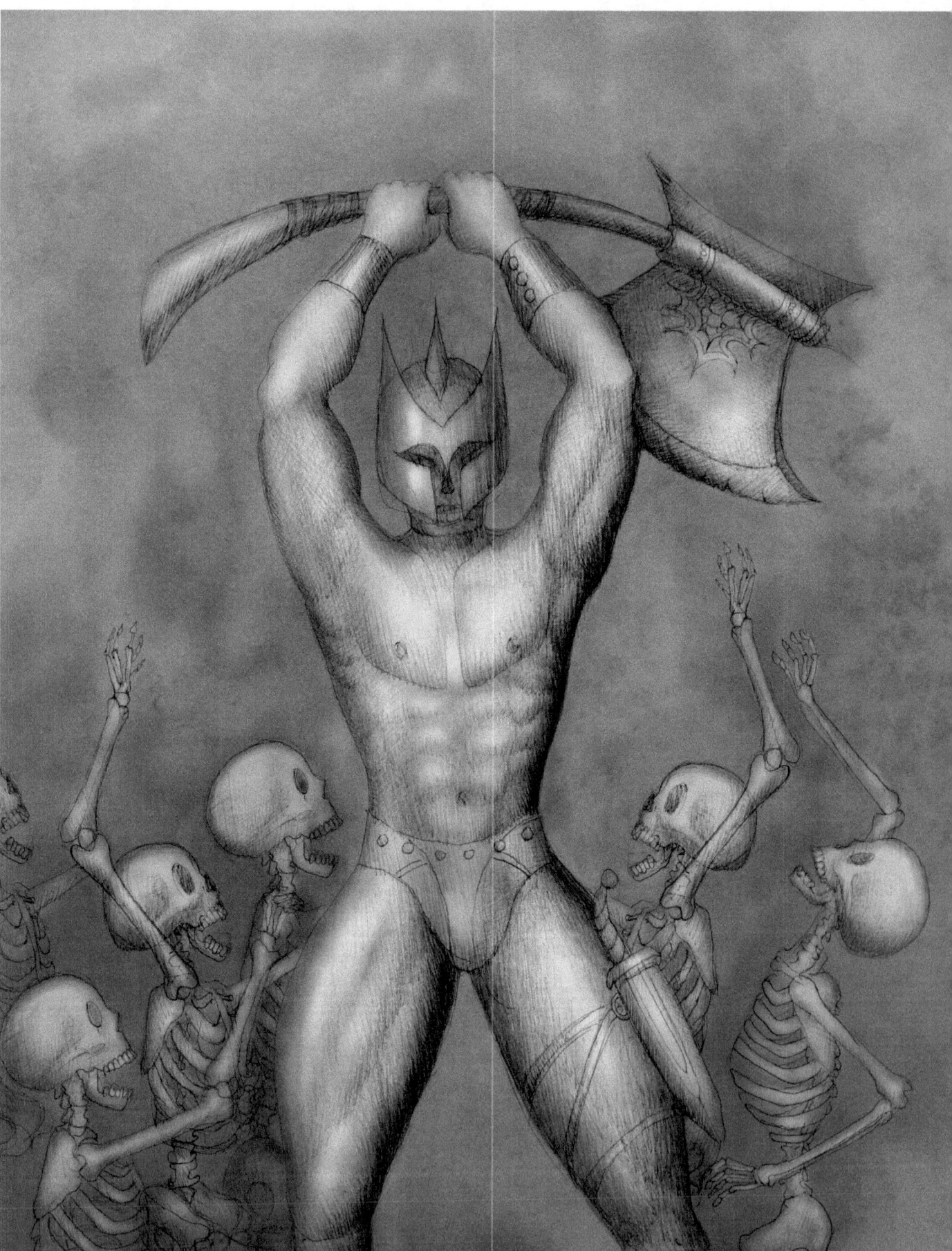

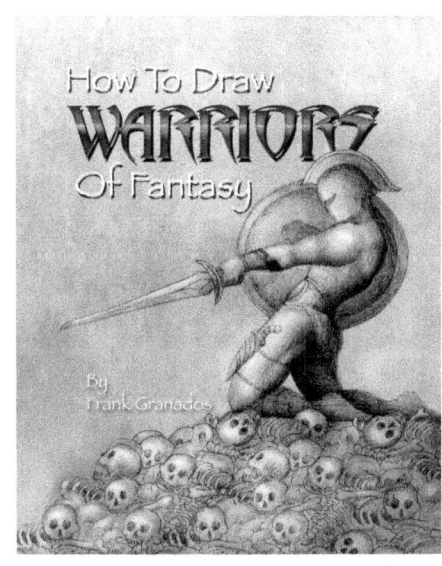

Also available

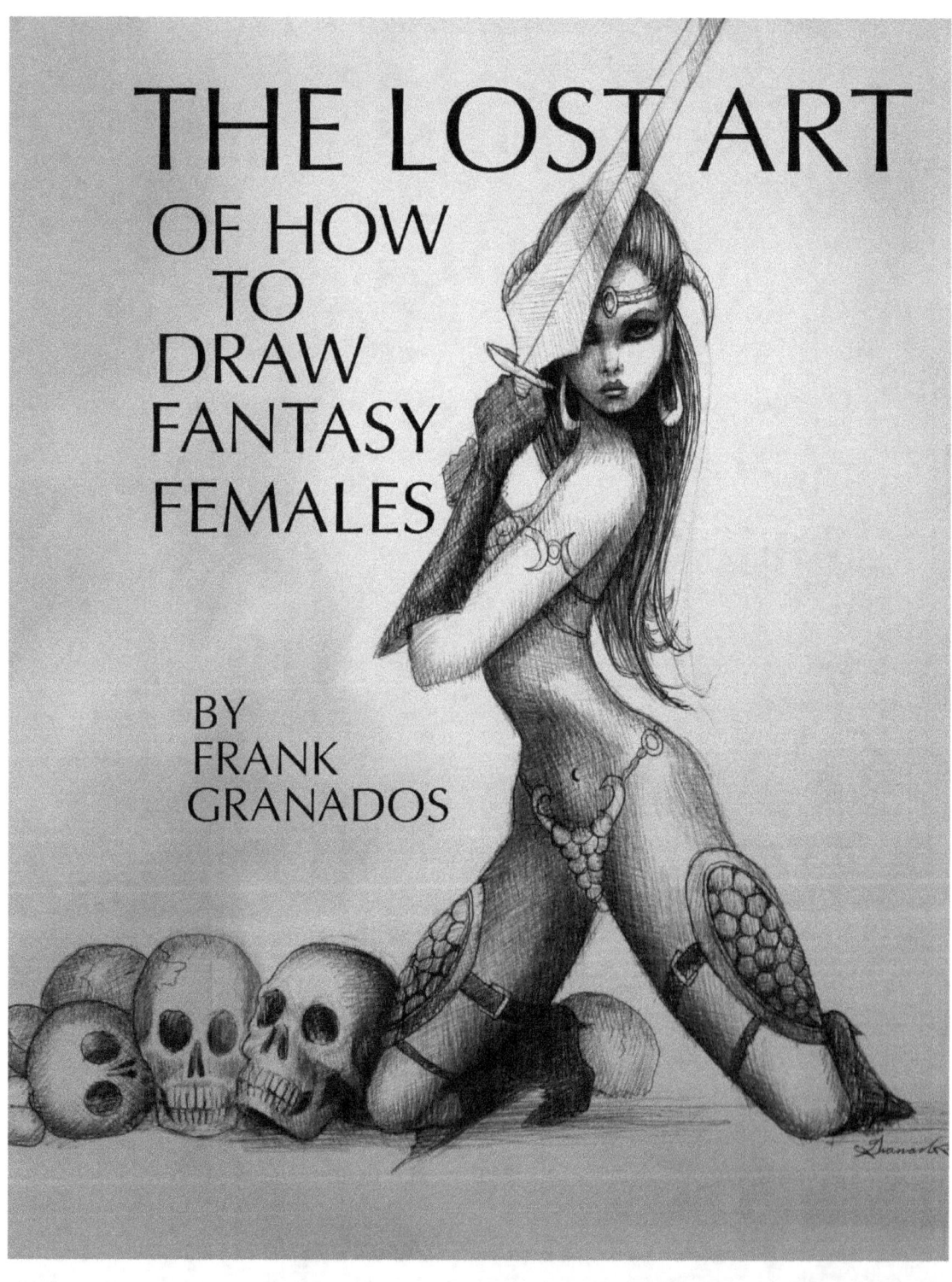

Also available

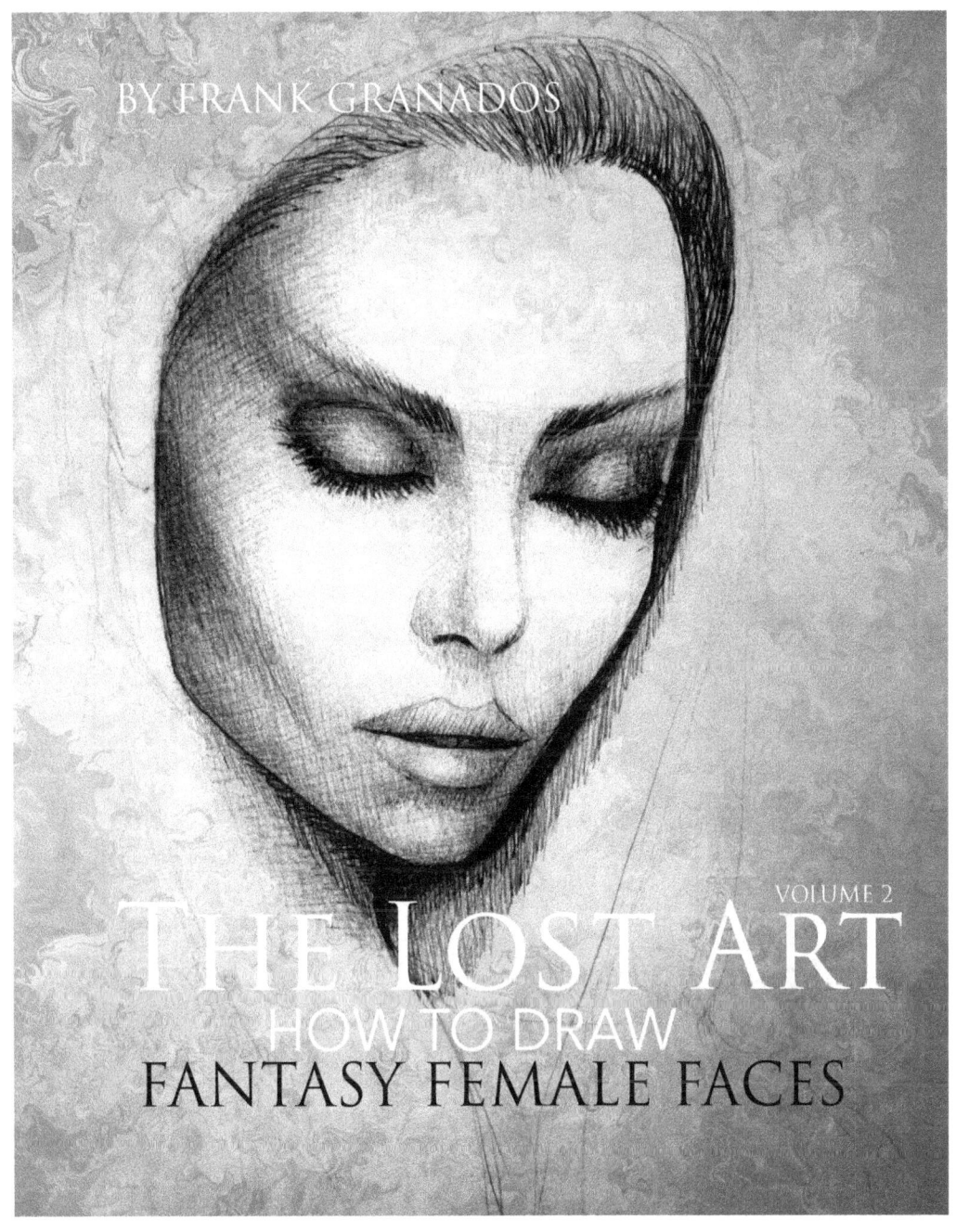

BY FRANK GRANADOS

VOLUME 2
THE LOST ART
HOW TO DRAW
FANTASY FEMALE FACES

coming soon

Vigo and the Dragon

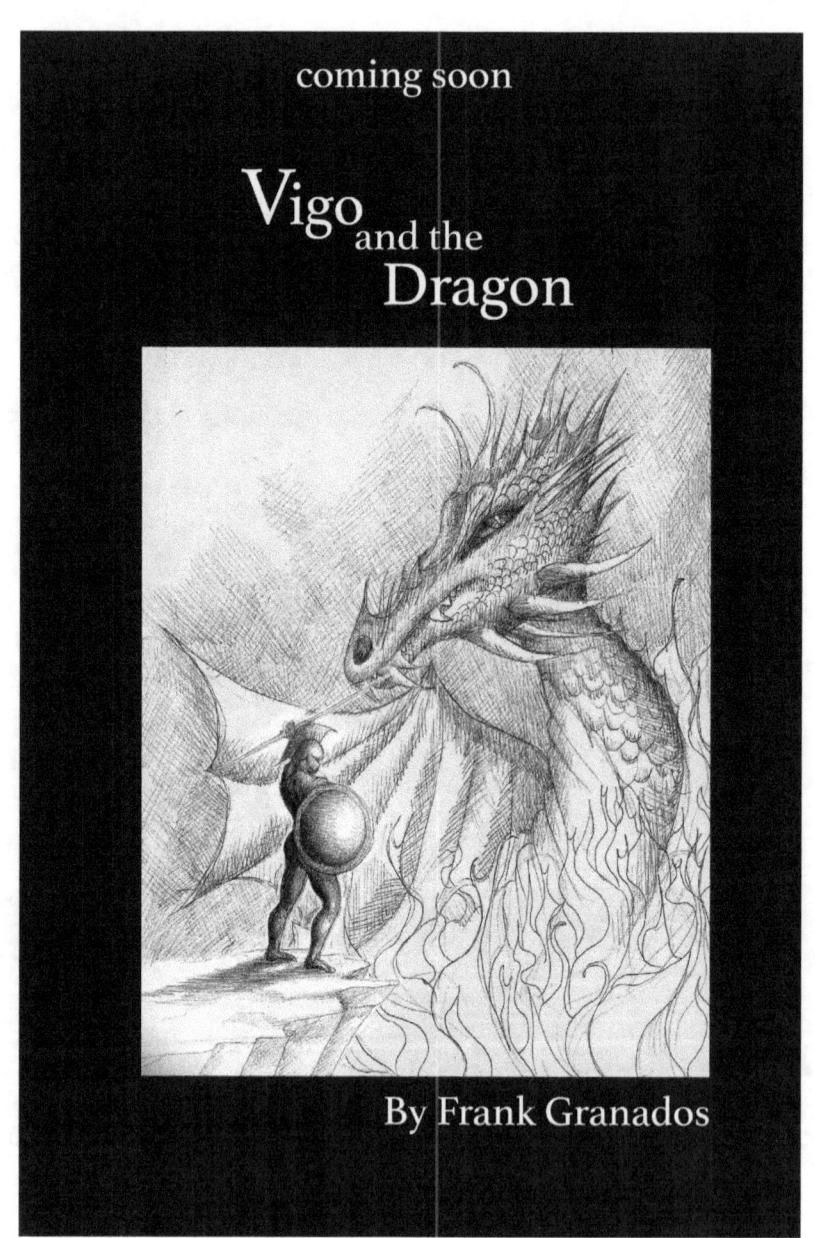

By Frank Granados